TROUBLE FINDS LITTLE MISS PERFECT

SHELLEY NOEL

CONTENTS

1. Speak Up — 1
2. The Early Years — 5
3. High School — 9
4. Shelley Becomes an Adult — 13
5. Prince Charming — 19
6. No Eye Contact. Bye Steph. Bye Grandpa. Hello, Wedding — 23
7. A Wedding, A Death. A Life — 31
8. Here Comes the Money! — 37
9. The Separation and My Mom — 43
10. Tom and Agent Rob — 49
11. Indicted — 55
12. Arrested — 61
13. "I'll Figure it out!" — 71
14. Chaos and Jesus — 75
15. Before The Trial — 81
16. The Beginning of the End! — 89
17. The Trial — 93
18. The Verdict — 97
19. Bond Hearing — 101
20. Civil War — 105
21. The Aftermath — 111
22. Chad's Sentencing Hearing — 117
23. My Sentence Hearing — 123
24. New Normal — 127

A Special Note From The Heart — 131
About the Author — 133
Acknowledgements — 135

DEDICATION

This book is dedicated to my boys. I am grateful God picked me to be your Mom. I hope I have shown you that you can overcome any adversity that comes your way. There is always a solution.

CHAPTER ONE
SPEAK UP

If you've ever been in a relationship with a narcissist, you'll know what I mean when I say how I often had to devalue myself, shrink or disappear so he could get the attention. Instead of having me walk into a room full of confidence, smiling at people, and being friendly, I was forced to not talk to anyone, not look at anyone, look down, and smile and nod in agreement as he told everyone how amazing he was. I was living in hell, and what made it worse was that I didn't know it.

It's hard to see the truth about a situation when you're in it. I was always loyal, had a great work ethic, and wanted my marriage to succeed. In other words, I just wanted to be the best wife I could be. As you read my story, you'll see I came from a broken home. My husband and I had two boys. The last thing I wanted to do was break up my family. The really crazy part is that everyone thought we were the perfect couple and I was living a fairytale life.

I was always told, "You are always so well put together!" Some friends would tease me good-naturedly by calling me Little Miss Perfect! I didn't intend to be perceived that way; I was just brought up by an immature mother and loving but strict and old-fashioned grandparents who taught me not to share my problems with anyone.

1

I'd always arrive places early, prepared, with a smile like I didn't have a care in the world, and people thought I had the best life and would have a fantastic life.

The sad truth was that I was a prisoner in my own home and my husband was the jailer. However, from the outside looking in – we had the perfect family. I get why they thought that. My husband and I became very successful. We had millions of dollars in assets: homes, cars, trucks, boats, and even an exotic ranch with horses, deer, zebra, buffalo, and rams!

So, when they saw us together or apart, and me carrying a new Louis Vuitton purse over my right shoulder, a massive rock on my ring finger, and a new Rolex watch on my left hand, getting out of whatever new SUV or car I was driving at the time, it would be easy to think we had it made. Little did they know, had I not thought I'd lose my boys, I would have traded places with any of them.

We had all of life's luxuries, but I wasn't the big spender; my husband was. He bought me the bags and watches and cars. When we had to turn over the ranch and other properties to the Trustee's, he started purchasing Quarter Horses – compact but versatile horses that competed in cutting competition. While I was busy on weekends taking the boys to birthday parties, games, practices, and extra curricular activities, he, accompanied by the long-term girl-friend I didn't know he had at the time, competed at cutting horse competitions.

"Watch. I'm going to be a world champion cutter!" He'd say.

"Yes, you will." I'd quickly agree, lest he think I thought he wouldn't, and start yelling at me.

He once paid $95K for one Quarter Horse! That's not counting the $1,400 monthly to stable each horse, of which we had five! That's also not including the monthly fee the horse trainer charged. But that was my husband. He made the money, he could spend it on whatever he wanted. I had little to no say - ever.

Take it from someone who has had many zeroes in her bank account – money does not buy happiness. Our younger son, Cole, once got a ride home from his boxing coach. I was outside and heard the coach say, "Wow, you have a nice house!" My son replied,

"It looks really good from the outside, but it's totally different inside." Cole was eleven years old. Even though we tried hard not to argue in front of the boys, they knew something was wrong.

I should have seen the signs. For instance, before we got married, if we were at a bar or club and a guy would accidentally brush by me, my husband would physically fight him. I would find out much later that he had been taking steroids and other drugs, but I didn't know it at the time. He would cause disturbances and scenes to the point that we got kicked out of restaurants, bars, clubs, and many other places we would go to. He would tell me that his problem was that he loved me so much, and it made him over-protective.

One time, I saw a co-worker at a restaurant and didn't dare say hello to him, fearing that my husband would beat him up or cause a scene. Also, being in that type of marriage made me think I would get his wife mad at him. That's what happens when you live with a narcissist, you think it's normal and everyone thinks the way they do. To keep the peace with everyone, I wouldn't talk to anyone from the opposite sex. It would set him off if he ever saw – or thought he saw - me having brief eye contact with another man!

His "over-protectiveness" alienated me from my best friend. With my sister living in a different country and growing up the way I did, that we suppress our emotions and didn't tell people what goes on at home – I was alone. I never talked about it, partly because I was raised that way but also because I had no one to talk to. For him not to get incredibly angry and volatile, I had to swallow my words and agree with him. After all, he knew everything, or so he would say. If an expert on something had a different opinion than him, we would fire them or not talk to them since he knew more.

Sure, with fair skin and blonde hair, I looked like Barbie and had all her toys, but my Ken was a monster. His ego knew no limits, and that was before we started making millions of dollars and getting invited to places where only those in high society are granted access. However, as you'll see, somehow, someway, God always made a way for me.

This book contains a crazy-but-absolutely-true story of a good girl who married a bad guy. You may think my calling him a bad guy may be my biased opinion; however, the state of Texas agrees with me as he now sits in prison trying to outlive his 45-year prison sentence – the same fate that awaited me had my faith in God wavered.

My future was dark. I couldn't see us getting out of the unbelievable position my husband put us in. My only solace was going for a run, listening to faith-based podcasts, and believing wholeheartedly that there had to be something better for me on the other side.

I'm no longer scared. I'm sharing the good, the bad, and the ugly of my life because someone who has not spoken up needs to know that it's okay for them to talk about it.

Finally, after many years of torture and feelings of isolation, I get to speak up.

CHAPTER TWO
THE EARLY YEARS

I was born east of Dallas, in Garland, Texas. My mother had me when she was 20, after having my sister, Heather, when she was 18 – we were born 14 months apart. My mother was young and immature when she had us, and in making sure I keep the truth, the truth, she got older but stayed immature for most of our lives, although, to her credit, after surviving her 2nd heart surgery, she became a different person, turned her life to God, and was a wonderful grandmother to her grandchildren.

Mom got pregnant both times while using an IUD – an Intra-Uterine Device (a T-shaped plastic the size of a quarter, placed inside her uterus to prevent pregnancy). IUDs are reported to be 99% effective, which, according to the healthcare community, makes Heather and I miracle babies!

My mother was also a miracle baby in that she had a successful open-heart surgery when she was three years old. She lived with the surgery scar on her shoulder blade for the rest of her life. She was told that, as she grew older, she would require the surgery again and that, due to her condition, she would never have children. Even with all of that, AND the IUDs, my sister and I were born… like I said, miracle babies.

Her parents, my grandparents, babied her as much as they could. They never wanted her to stress, fearing she would need open-heart surgery again. With her being their only daughter, (she had a brother), and them overcompensating her for her heart condition, they didn't give her a lot of responsibility growing up. That might have meant a lot of fun for her growing up but it doesn't have the makings of a great mom once she has children.

My mother – Debbie Rush married my dad – James Tollison, often referred to as a bastard because his mother was not married to his father when he was born, which was a big deal in the 1950's in the south. My dad's mother had four other children over the years and was married to their fathers. My mother met him in high school and ran off with him, not telling her parents she had gotten married. Heather and I think she did it out of spite or rebellion towards her parents.

My mother's parents were solid, hard-working people. My grandfather was the president of a bank for a long time. Then, he owned a real estate brokerage and opened a sporting goods store, selling fishing equipment, guns, and anything related to hunting and fishing; including hunting and fishing licenses. Grandpa's sporting store evolved into a pawnshop because of his big heart. People who couldn't pay would trade things that had nothing to do with hunting or fishing, so he started selling those items, and his store morphed into a pawnshop.

My grandfather had an excellent reputation. He owned eight rental properties and picked up the rent checks in person weekly. However, if someone didn't have the total rent, for whatever reason, he would dismiss what he or she owed and collect what he or she could without ever having to pay it afterward.

My grandparents didn't like that my dad was a bastard, but that's not why they didn't like him. According to them, Dad was a pot-smoking hippie who preferred to complain about the government and would do more fishing than working. He certainly did not check the important boxes for him to marry their only daughter, whom they had taken great care of to raise. My dad never knew his father. His mother chose his last name from a guy she was dating at the time of his birth – not his actual biological father. So, my sister and I had no blood or legal ties to our last name. I have no idea who Mr. Tollison is or was and whose name we carried until our marriages.

My mother, who was raised getting her way, got sick of her non-working, always fishing husband and left him when Heather was three and I was two. Her parents had been telling her that while she was married to that deadbeat hippie, they wouldn't help her financially, but if she were to leave him, they would help. True to their word, they started to help Mom financially, and she never went back with him.

He would often say he was going to see his daughters but would never make it. Heather had gotten to the age where she would wait and wait and wait for him, only for him not to show up and for her to go to bed crying. Mom finally gave him an ultimatum, "We don't have to get back together but be a full-time dad or nothing at all!" Apparently, he saw it as a way out of fatherly responsibilities and never returned. "I really thought he would step up!" she told us many years later. *I ended up meeting my biological father when I was 20.*

My mother worked as a dental assistant for different dentists for almost 30 years. We would move from apartment to apartment. She was already gone for work before we woke up for school. Heather and I had to get ourselves dressed, make our breakfasts, walk to school, walk back home from school, and fend for ourselves again for food until she got home tired from work. There was no order, no structure, and no schedule. Some days, we would decide we didn't want to go through the hassle of getting ourselves ready and would not go to school and our mother would never find out.

Mom would take us shopping every weekend, but not necessarily for us. She would buy a new outfit every week to go out on Saturday nights. She wasn't heavily into drugs like my biological father, but she would drink on weekends. She would go out, have a boyfriend for a while, usually a biker. The guy would inevitably use her or she would offer to buy him gifts using her credit cards, ring her credit cards up to the max, cry to her parents, and they would pay them off so it would not ruin her credit. It was cyclical chaos, time after time.

Mom would take us to different houses and parties. It was usually a Harley-riding biker party. She would join in the festivities — pot smoking or drinking or both, dancing, laughing, and having a grand old time and pretty much leave Heather and me on our own. So, my sister and I would run around and notice the difference in how the adults acted from when they arrived, clear-headed and when they left; slurring, stumbling, and the occasional person that got carried to a bed because he or she passed out. Watching that made me never want to do drugs and do the crazy things they would do while drunk or high. It formed me into a rule follower. I became a routine-oriented person. I just wanted to do the right thing and not rock any boats.

One of the worst parts of my upbringing was being in the car with mom. She was a poor driver at best and caused many accidents. If we made her mad while in the car, she would purposefully drive like a crazy woman to scare us. One time in the evening, she accidentally drove into a brick wall while we were in the car. It would have been a funny story had Heather not broken an arm and suffered from a swollen brain to the point that they thought she needed brain surgery! Thankfully, my sister didn't have brain damage and didn't suffer any long-term effects. My mother hurt her shoulder badly. Thankfully for me, I didn't get a scratch.

Middle school is a blur now. I had the typical middle school experience. My hormones changed, I started liking boys, and kissed my first boy in 7th grade! Mostly, I did what everyone in my middle school did for fun, roller-skating.

I had no idea what to expect when I got to high school, but I certainly didn't expect to get raped!

CHAPTER THREE
HIGH SCHOOL

I started working out and running at around 16. No one else in my family did it, but I was drawn to it and loved it. As an adult now, I realize it was partly a coping mechanism or a way to escape, as some people might do drugs, drink, or gamble. My grandparents raised us to believe it was more proper to keep your emotions in. "You don't spill the beans," they'd say. It was a safe environment for sure; it's not like they did terrible things to us that they wanted us to keep from everyone, it was more of a mindset towards life they grew up believing. So, I learned early on that if anyone said anything rude to me or anything out of the ordinary happened, I was supposed to keep it to myself.

I started dating one particular boy from another high school. I met him through my best friend, Stacie, who was dating one of his friends. They were both on the baseball team and I would accompany Stacie to their home games. He was good-looking and athletic. This was before social media, so he asked for my phone number, which I gave, and he started calling me. Then, we started hanging out with Stacie and her boyfriend and then by ourselves. He invited me to his house to watch TV and hang out. I went to the apartment he lived in with his mother, but she wasn't there.

9

We hadn't known each other too long, and I was still a virgin; I certainly did not go there with the intention of having sex – at all. Remember, I was a rule follower, a goody-two-shoes.

He greeted me with a kiss, which I happily returned, and led me to the sofa. After a little while, I pulled back, wondering if we were going to watch TV or do anything, but his mind was made up. He touched my knee a little aggressively and started to move his hand up my leg. I got nervous, but I liked him and, although I stopped his hand, we started kissing again. Then, out of nowhere, he tried to lift my shirt! He didn't ask me or anything! I pulled away and told him I wasn't ready for that. He said some sweet-nothings in my ear, and I smiled, which empowered him to try to take my shirt off again. I forcefully removed his hands, and that's when he changed.

He grabbed me and roughly laid me on the sofa. I kept telling him that we weren't ready, that I wasn't ready, that I was saving myself, that I wanted my first time to be special, and many different ways of telling him I did not want to have sex. However, he startled me and roughly grabbed my shoulders to the point that pain shot through my body.

I was alone and felt utterly defenseless as he pulled my pants and underwear down. I kept trying to pick them up, but he was much stronger than me. Before I realized it, he began raping me as I kept telling him to get off of me. It was painful and violent.

Although it felt like it lasted a lifetime, thankfully, in real time, it didn't last long. He got off of me, and I stood up quickly to pull my pants up. I saw blood streaming down my legs and thought to glare at him or yell at him, but I didn't want to provoke him. As soon as I put my clothes on, I headed for the door, in fear that he would grab me again or try to talk to me to apologize, which I would not have accepted, but it didn't matter; he didn't do either. In the end, he raped me and I walked out without either of us saying a word.

I thought about telling the authorities, my grandparents, or my sister, but only briefly. Back then, if a girl went to a popular boy's house, you had no defense. They'd shame you, call you a whore, and blame it on you. I didn't want that type of spotlight on me. Also, at around that time, many stories were coming out in Hollywood of women being sexually assaulted by rich and powerful men. Most people didn't believe the victim, and I certainly did not want to be ridiculed. So, I went home and went on with my day and life.

I never cried. I never had anxiety attacks. I never had nightmares about it. Nothing. It happened. It was awful. But it was over, and talking to anyone about it would make it last forever. The good thing was that he went to another high school, and I never saw him again. Little did I know that I was being groomed to become the type of woman that would attract a narcissistic predator.

Life went on, with my grandparents instilling a good work ethic into us. We mowed the lawn, helped change the oil, helped with the plants, picked the vegetables from the garden and washed them – whatever needed to be done, we did it. My sister would often fight with my mother. She would get upset because my grandmother waited on our mother hand and foot. Grandma would do Mom's laundry, give her money, and babied her her entire life. Meanwhile, we did chores during the school year and helped out at the pawnshop during the summers.

I sort of dated several boys from my school, but nothing serious. I made sure never to put myself in a bad situation again and once the boys realized I wouldn't be alone with them, things ended quickly. I fell hard for someone when I was a junior. I saw him at a few high school parties, and we took a liking to each other. Like most boys, he would drink hard, but I was never a big drinker. It would be a crazy night for me if I finished one wine cooler. I had no idea my new boyfriend was starting to get hooked on drugs.

One minute, he'd be calling me non-stop, wanting to hang out, and the next day, he would disappear, and I wouldn't hear a peep from him in two or three days. After confronting him on some of his bizarre actions, he broke down and cried and told me he had a drug addiction. I've always been a "fixer," so instead of running away, I went deeper with him, trying to help him and bail him out of situations. Again, looking back at it as an adult, that's probably what my mother used to do. He had the same characteristics and behaviors that my mother's boyfriends had. He was a couple of years older than me, so he had already graduated.

He started showing up to "pick me up" from school, which I thought was sweet. But then he started showing up drunk or fidgety and would make a scene over the littlest things. My friends and even some teachers told me to be careful with him and to walk away from him but I told them they didn't know him like I did, and that I could take care of myself. His antics at school didn't stop, but instead of leaving him, I left the school.

I went to a small private school, but he did the same things there. I loved him and wanted to help him so badly and believed I could. I left that small, private school and went to night school, where primarily girls went that got pregnant or in trouble. I graduated from high school but never experienced a high school graduation.

I didn't "blossom" until after high school. I was in gymnastics for two years and was thin and super flexible. I had a growth spurt and got up to 5'6, which essentially led me to stop doing gymnastics. Many of my friends were cheerleaders, but I never got much attention.

With school behind me and a working life ahead of me, I knew I had to make a change, I certainly didn't want him to ruin my career as he did my high school years. Even though I had feelings for him, enough had been enough and I broke up with him. I was optimistic about my future, wherever it was and with whoever it may have been with.

CHAPTER FOUR

SHELLEY BECOMES AN ADULT

TIME TO BE AN ADULT

My friend Stacie got me a job at a popular and growing insurance company. I had been working since I was 15 but this felt like my first real job. It was busy and demanding but also a ton of fun because everyone got along. A large group of us would eat lunch together and hang out after work and on weekends. We'd go to dinners, Country Western bars, and wherever we could do some country dancing. I got to reconnect with friends I hadn't seen since I left high school. Life was simple but fun.

While dancing one night, a tall, muscular, good-looking man asked me to dance. He didn't do it very macho, it was almost as if he was fighting his shyness. I thought it was the cutest thing ever. We danced a few times, with me dancing with others in between, and I left hoping to see him again because he didn't ask for my number. I saw him two weeks later and he practically ran up to me.

"Hey, slow down partner," I shouted.

"I wanted to make sure I got to you before anyone else asked you to dance. Shall we?"

Unlike the first night, he didn't give me a chance to dance with anyone else that night. Not that I minded, I was starting to discover I had a "type," and he fit the mold perfectly: smart, kind, athletically built, tall, and respectful.

FROM BOYS TO MEN

We started dating and although I was still living with my grandparents, I would stay at his apartment often. He had a busy schedule, being that he was going to college to get an engineering degree, and he worked full-time. When we did have time, we would go to concerts, movies, watch sporting events – this Dallas girl loves her Cowboys and Mavericks – and, of course, go dancing!

He was a sweet guy and we fell for each other. He told me that his mother left his father because he had been physically abusive towards her. He was very close and protective of his mom, which is probably why he found time to work out often. Actually, we often worked out together. He was totally against the mistreatment of women. He won my sister over easily, and not even Grandma or Grandpa could not like him. Mind you, I had put them through the wringer with my druggie high school boyfriend, so this guy was an angel compared to him.

After two years we started having more meaningful conversations about our future. We had talked about it before, but being that we celebrated our second anniversary, it was time to talk about it again. He had always said that he didn't know if he'd ever want to have kids but was positive, he didn't ever want to get married when we met. However, those viewpoints could change when you're in love with someone who does.

Unfortunately, even though he told me he loved me and couldn't see a happy life without me, he doubled down on not wanting to get married.

"I mean, maybe you can convince me to have kids, but after growing up watching my parents hate their lives while they were together, I just won't get married."

Maybe I could convince him to have kids? But for what, to have kids out of wedlock?

Now, at that time, I wasn't religious, even though I spent a year in a Christian school, but if and when I had children, I wanted to have them through the sanctity of a marriage. As I had mentioned in an earlier chapter, my father was a bastard when it was a bad thing in the south, and I certainly didn't want my children to go through any of that.

I stayed with him because I did love him, but the nagging feeling that I'd never be married or may never have children started to become a hefty weight on my mind and spirit. After another year, just after celebrating our third anniversary, I told him I couldn't do it anymore. He was devastated, but, as I stuck to my convictions, so did he. We parted ways amicably and moved on with our lives.

My family was sorry that we broke up, but they also knew I'd never be happy long-term if he didn't want to marry. "There are a lot of good fellas out there that would jump at the chance to see you walking towards them on the aisle; you'll be okay." My grandpa said. He always did have a way with words.

I joined the single friend's pool and began hanging out again. People told me I was a catch because I was beautiful, blonde, made my own money, was easy to make laugh, and very fit. It lifted my spirits, but even though some really cute guys would ask me out, I wasn't ready. Until I met Nick, a former Mr. Texas Body Builder winner.

Nick was five years older than me and owned a gym in a nearby town. I met him through a friend of a friend, and we started a casual conversation that I thought wouldn't amount to anything. Then, we started working out together and before I knew it, I was dating someone again. I really did have a type! He was tall, intelligent, and checked all the boxes. I didn't see it early on, but he was really into himself. However, you don't win Mr. Texas if you're not into yourself, so it didn't bother me enough to break up with him.

We never moved in with each other, but I'd stay over occasionally, less often than when I was in my previous relationship, but this was a different relationship. Nick loved three things – working out, vacationing, and gambling in Vegas – and we would do those three

15

things together as often as we could, except I wouldn't gamble nearly as hard as he would.

The weeks turned into months, and the months turned into a year, and that year turned into two years, and the third year was on the horizon when we had "the talk" about our future. I told him I really wanted to get married and have kids. Like the previous guy, Nick did not want to get married. "I don't think I could ever be ready for that level of commitment, Shell." For the first time in my life, someone broke up with me. Personally, I was devastated. Financially, things had improved.

MOVING ON UP

I had left the insurance job in good standing and got a job as an office manager somewhere else. By the way, I'm still great friends with many of my co-workers at the insurance company. The opportunity to move up from a receptionist to an office manager was appealing, even though the owner turned out to be quite odd.

He later told me that when I went to the interview and was waiting to be called into his office, he went out the back door to look at my car to see if it was clean. If it were unkempt, he would have never hired me. However, being that my grandparents taught me always to be neat, tidy, and orderly, my car passed his inspection, and I got the job.

I was in my early-20s, and he was in his late 50s; however, that didn't stop him from trying to bed me. He always dated young pretty women. However, if I'm honest – I always thought they were trashy looking. Every single one of them was bleach blond, big (sometimes fake) boobs, and wore skimpy clothes and high heels. It was evident that he had a type too. As for him, he was old and looked old and wasn't very good-looking. His charm was that he had a ton of family money and a thriving business.

After working there for a year, turning down his sloppy, sometimes borderline vulgar advances, and ignoring his "compliments," he gave me a proposal. When I wrote, he gave me a proposal, I mean, he actually wrote a contract for me to sign. The proposal stated that he would double my salary, give me a vehicle, I'd have access to his credit cards, and live at his house rent-free. The stipulation was that I had to be his girlfriend! Not just a trophy-wife-type girlfriend that he could show off in public, he wanted the full girlfriend experience with me.

I read the contract and had mixed emotions. I didn't know if I should have been insulted and slapped him or if I should have laughed. I didn't do either. I told him, "I'm going to say this once. No. Straight up. I'm not for sale. This is not open for negotiation or discussion. Just, no. Now, leave my office and let me get this paperwork done or fire me." He walked out of the office, and I continued working there as if nothing had happened. We ended up being good work friends, even though he couldn't stop asking me for drinks or dinner from time to time, which I always respectfully rejected.

THE FAMILY

On the home front, much had changed. When I was 24, Mom, who was 44 and had lived quite the life, had to have open-heart surgery. She prayed earnestly to God, saying, "God, I know I've been far from perfect. But I'm so scared of this surgery. If you get me through this, I promise I'll turn my life over to you completely." God kept up his end of the bargain and Mom recuperated nicely from the surgery. Heather and I didn't gamble often, but if we had to bet, we would have put every penny that our mother would not live up to her part of the bargain. To our surprise, we would have lost our money! Our mother did a total one-eighty. She left her old friends, started going to church regularly, joined a bible study group, stopped drinking, and became an entirely different person.

For all our lives, Mom was an okay mother, but she did love partying and kept hooking up with the wrong men to the point we had to live with her parents. In saying that, 24 years of my life passed that she could never take back and be a better mother or role model. However, once she made that prayer, she got much more into the family. She would later become an exceptional grandmother whose grandkids loved and adored.

17

She would later retire from the dental industry and open her pet-sitting business. She would take my older son walking and caring for and feeding dogs, which he loved. But, I'm getting ahead of myself.

While still in her 20s, my sister Heather married a great guy. He was a wiz within the tech community. However, on September 11, better known as 9/11 in 2001, al-Qaeda carried out four coordinated Islamic suicide terrorist attacks against the United States. If you were alive when that happened, you know how the temperate of America changed, especially towards people from the Middle East. Heather's husband, the great guy and tech wiz, was half Arabic and had an Arabic last name.

He had a terrible time finding employment, regardless of his talent. They were forced to leave the country due to unemployment and he got a job in Cairo, which resulted in my sister and life-long confidant moving out of the country at the time I got engaged.

So there I was, not realizing I was at a crossroads in my life. I had been through two three-year relationships that ended. I was working for a quirky old man who wanted to bed me, and my sister had left the country.

Not long after, I met Chad.

CHAPTER FIVE
PRINCE CHARMING

I was single but happy. I had two different three-year relationships that ended due to the issue of marriage, and wasn't ready for another one, especially if the outcome were to be the same. I continued to work and hang out with friends, thinking I'd put the dating thing off for a while.

Tisha was one of the friends I hung out with. I met her because she was dating one of Nick's close friends when I was dating Nick, and we found ourselves hanging out often, which was a bonus as she was fun to be around. She called me to see if I wanted to hang out. She had broken up with Nick's friend and was meeting a guy she was interested in and some of his friends. "You have to come with me. I don't want to be the only girl with him and all his friends," she pleaded.

I met up with her at a popular Country Western bar in Dallas and shortly after that, the guy she was talking to arrived. Little by little, his friends started to show up. Most were "gym" guys and a few were quite cute. She introduced me to each one as they came in, and we'd chat it up until I got introduced to the next guy that showed up, and then I'd talk to that person.

One particular guy looked at me so hard I thought he looked

19

through me. "Hey, I'm Chad," he said, without waiting to be introduced. We started to converse, you know, the basics: *What do you do? Do you live in Dallas? Have you been here before?*

It turned out that Chad was two years younger than me, which would have been a red flag until he told me he served in the military, had a chemical engineering degree, and was already a homeowner. I thought he was a solid guy and already established at his age. The next guy came in and Tisha interrupted my conversation with Chad to introduce me, but instead of me talking to the new guy, Chad turned me back to him and kept talking with me. I thought it was a confident move from the youngster. Soon after, the bar got jam-packed and the only way to talk to someone was to yell.

"Let's go outside and talk!" He shouted.

"What?"

He got closer to my left ear and nonchalantly put his left hand on my hip. "I said, let's go outside and talk!"

"You know what?" I yelled. "I can't hear you well, let's talk outside!"

We ended up talking in his truck for a while. I discovered he was from Oklahoma and had only been in Dallas for less than a year. He told me he had served in the Navy for four years and had earned a degree in Chemical Engineering. A few things were pretty evident; he was confident, intelligent, charismatic, good-looking, and into me. He had a lot of stability for a 25-year-old, which every girl likes. However, he also told me he was married and in the middle of a divorce. Even though that was a little red flag, he assured me his relationship with his first wife was over, so we exchanged numbers at the end of the night.

He had some great qualities but was in the middle of a divorce. What if he never wanted to get married again? What if he did something terrible to the wife he's divorcing?

He called me at least five times in the following three weeks. I found his pursuit of me admirable. After the fifth call, I called him back and noticed I immediately had his undivided attention. We agreed to go out – actually, he would not take no for an answer, so I agreed to let him take me out. He was the picture-perfect gentleman. He got out and opened the door for me. As I got in his truck, he brought me beautiful flowers and took me to a nice restaurant.

He was a great conversationalist and did not fear being the center of attention. He was quick-witted and chatted up the hostess and got us a seat before others who had gotten there earlier than we did.

I went home thinking this young man had it all together. He had a good-paying job, he had a college degree, he had impeccable manners, he was intelligent, outgoing, good-looking, and in great shape. His truck was always clean and he even color-coded the clothes in his closet! What else did a Dallas girl need?

We became inseparable after our first date. He would almost always have a gift for me, a trinket of some sort, whether it was a necklace, bracelet, or something else. It was evident that he thought of me when we weren't together. Our first kiss was my gratitude for him getting me adorable small diamond earrings before our date. Trust me when I tell you, that kiss passed the fireworks test. He was so into me it made me feel like Wonder Woman. We went out alone, with his friends, with my friends, or with my sister and her boyfriend. He was like a cat in the sense that whatever circle I threw him in, he'd land on his feet.

Little did I know that his job wasn't paying him as much as he eluded, and he was getting deep into debt while wining and dining me. He looked stressed on one particular date, and when I pressed him to confide in me, he told me that the house he was selling was in his and his ex-wife's name and because they only had it for just one year, they had no equity in it. They had to pay the realtor and the closing costs, and he didn't have the few thousand on his end to pay his half, so his ex-wife had to pay it so they could get out of the house.

So, here he was, taking me to the most expensive dinners in the area, but on the other hand, he was hemorrhaging money. I told him I was a simple girl and he didn't have to go all out for me but he insisted on giving me "the best money can buy." What can I say? I fell for Prince Charming. Hard.

Looking back at it now, perhaps it was because of all the gifts and unwavering attention, I didn't notice some things that I'd quickly pick up from anyone else. For example, he would speak for me at times, which I never needed anyone to do. If someone asked me a question, whether it be a friend or a waitress, he'd answer for me. It didn't bother me, though. I thought he was being chivalrous, and I never checked him on it because he was smart and wouldn't sound stupid.

After six remarkable months of dating, we agreed to move in together – actually, he wouldn't take no for an answer. I had two long-term boyfriends but never moved in with them, but Prince Chad was an entirely different breed. We moved into a great one-bedroom apartment in Plano, Texas, and settled in.

Cinderella and Prince Charming had found their castle, and I eagerly anticipated a new, wonderful life.

CHAPTER SIX

NO EYE CONTACT. BYE STEPH. BYE GRANDPA. HELLO, WEDDING

I thought perhaps living with a man for the first time would be a significant change, but the truth is I would spend a lot of time at his place, so the process of being with him daily was pretty smooth. It was a small apartment but that didn't matter because we weren't there that often.

I was working full-time and he was working at Air Liquide, a French-based company that provided industrial gases and services to various industries. Chad's position required him to travel and help build semiconductors. He had to wear operating room-type clothing and, among many other things, ensure that the temperature didn't get above or below what would have affected the chemicals. It was very complicated and detailed work and I was proud of him for putting his engineering degree to good use.

I didn't like to cook. I've never been a big eater; I ate to survive; food was never a big part of who I was. I don't have one single memory of my mother cooking a homemade meal. My grandmother was the one who cooked. Chad, on the other hand, was an excellent cook. In fact, he was the only one who cooked in the house. He loved to grill and we ended up having huge cookouts later in life. But in the beginning, we would eat out a lot.

We spent every Sunday at my grandparents' house watching the Dallas Cowboys with my family. Chad, being from Oklahoma, had no family in Texas. However, he was friendly and outgoing and fit in with my family, and everyone else, like a glove. Weekends were mostly spent hanging out with friends.

The first six months went by fast – many restaurants, hanging out, watching the Cowboys, and working. We were in a blissful groove and I was thrilled with where my life was. We started talking more seriously about having kids in the future and building our own house. I finally found someone that wanted to get married one day! However, he had just gotten a divorce, so I made sure not to press him into it.

At around the six-month mark, I started to see chinks in Prince Charming's armor. I guess they were there from the very beginning, but I couldn't or wouldn't acknowledge them because he was sweeping me off my feet.

As you know by now, I have always been a gym girl and he was also very fit, so, as I did in previous relationships, we would go to the gym together. I grew up in the area, so I naturally had many friends and acquaintances. While at the gym, people would smile and nod, say hi, or wave hello from across the gym, to which I would reciprocate. Nothing crazy, right? Not for Chad. As soon as we'd be alone in the car, he would start in on me:

Who was that?
How do you know him?
I'm right next to you. Is he trying to disrespect me?
You better not encourage that guy. Hear me?
I saw how you were looking at him. What? Do you think I'm stupid?
I swear, Shell, if he does that again, I'm gonna kick his ass.
And what gives you the right to smile at guys when we're at the gym?
What else do you do when I'm not here?
What don't I know?
Are people laughing at me behind my back?
If you think you're ever going to this gym without me, you're stupider than I thought!

I don't know what I thought at first when he started behaving like this. Maybe I wanted to believe that he just loved me so much he didn't want any chance of losing me. I tried to tell him it was all in his head, but he would shut me down. Sometimes, he was terrifying, with his eyes bulging and veins popping out of his neck as he screamed at me in the parking lot of the gym.

I expected him to apologize for going overboard the first few times, especially since he was very kind and considerate to others. Yet, the apologies never came. If anything, he'd bring up our future and how committed he was to making me the happiest girl alive. Then, we'd have a great night out, eat, dance, laugh, and make love. I figured that maybe someone had cheated on him before and soon enough he'd realize I'm a one-man woman and I've never cheated on anyone and I loved him and would never cheat on him. That never happened. Instead, I had to change.

No matter where we were; the gym, grocery shopping, at a restaurant, in a bar or club, I had to make sure not to draw attention to myself. My heart would skip when an old school friend would spot me in a restaurant. If he would come to say hello and ask how I'd been, Chad would definitely flip out on me and there was a good chance he would flip out on the guy too. So, I got very good at avoiding eye contact and making myself invisible.

Due to my invisible ninja skills, we didn't fight a lot. However, I was always on high alert. I had to check my surroundings constantly. I figured the price of us not fighting and getting along was more than worth the effort. I became very submissive, something I saw from my mother with her boyfriends. I was the perfect match for Chad because he disliked sharing the spotlight. He had one of those big charismas, a presence that took over the room. People were drawn to him and wanted to be his friend. He could talk about anything – sports, business, church, politics, you name it. To be honest, I was okay with it. I never wanted the spotlight and had a man who could do a better job than me and handle it.

We went out one night and met up with Stephanie, my best friend. We were all quite tipsy and she asked if she could crash on our couch when we got in after two in the morning, which we said of course. Chad was hungry and wanted to go to Whataburger, but I was done for the night. Stephanie was hungry too, so they both left and I went to bed.

The following day, I realized Stephanie either didn't sleep on our couch or got up early and left. When I asked Chad, he said, "Who cares what she does? I keep telling you not to trust her. She's not who she says she is."

I didn't find the comment odd because he almost always had something negative to say about my friends. A few nights later, a mutual friend, Kathy, called me.

"Have you talked to Stephanie?" she asked.

"Not since we went out the other night. Why?"

"Well, I was struggling if I should tell you this because you and Chad are thinking of getting married, but I wouldn't be a good friend to you if I kept my mouth shut."

"Spill it already," I urged. "What's going on?"

"Apparently, when Chad and Stephanie went to the drive-thru, he came on to her."

"What?"

"She told me he tried to kiss her. She told him, 'You're about to marry my best friend. What is the matter with you?' So when she returned to your apartment, she felt uncomfortable and left." There was an uncomfortable pause. "I'm sorry to be telling you this. I hate being the bearer of bad news."

"Steph and I have been best friends since forever. Why are you telling me and not her?" Nothing was making sense.

"I don't know. Please don't be mad at me."

Chad was in the apartment, so I confronted him about it as soon as I hung up with Kathy.

"Stephanie said I came on to her? That lying bitch! She came on to me! I told you I never trusted her. We were in the drive-thru, got the food and she asked if we could go for a ride. I asked her for what and she gave me that slut look. She wanted to hook up with me but I came right home and told her she couldn't stay over."

Chad's enormous charisma and confidence were on full display. He could have won an Oscar for his performance. But what really bothered me was that Stephanie still hadn't called me. So, I called her.

"Shelley, listen to me. I would never do that to you. You know that. He tried to kiss me and I backed off and told him he was about to marry my best friend and how messed up that was. I didn't know what to do so I called Kathy."

"Since we're such good friends, why didn't you call me?" I asked, pissed off.

"I called Kathy for advice, and she told me not to tell you that he was probably just drunk and not worth ruining your wedding and your happiness. What else was I supposed to do? You know I've always been in your corner. He's lying."

"Don't call Chad a liar! He's been telling me not to trust you since he met you. He always knew you liked him."

"What? No! I promise you. I didn't do anything."

I had come to my conclusion. "Stephanie, I can't believe you did this to me. We've been like sisters since we were fourteen years old. If you had nothing to worry about, you would have told me. I even traveled with you and your family! I guess our friendship never meant that much to you. I don't need to talk to you anymore. Goodbye."

Stephanie was the first person he isolated me from. He knew that no matter what, she would always be in my corner. After that, he talked badly about her all the time. I know now it was in fear that she would convince me of the truth.

As I write this, there is no doubt in my mind that Chad made a move on her. He was a good-looking guy and wasn't used to being rejected and was scared no one would say anything, but since it came out to the light, he did everything in his power to convince me that he was this chick-magnet but no matter what, he'd always be loyal to me.

Soon after I lost my best friend, my grandfather passed away. He was the only father figure in my life and the pillar of our family. He had Parkinson's disease and had gotten to the point where my grandmother couldn't adequately care for him. He was six feet tall and strong, and Grandma was a tall, slim woman. She had to put him in a home to get the proper care. Every time I visited, he'd ask, beg me to take him out of there.

"Grandpa, you're going to be okay. You'll get used to this place, it's really nice. They're taking excellent care of you. You'll be fine. I promise," I'd say.

He didn't last four months. He gave up and stopped eating. His death was a monumental blow to the family, but probably most to me, as I was his closest grandchild. With my best friend out of the picture, Chad stepped up for me big time. He had liked my grandpa a lot and showed him a lot of respect, which made my grandpa like him a lot as well. We were all in mourning, but I was happy that Chad was there.

My grandma was hurting more than ever before. She too started showing signs of giving up and depended on me for many things. I helped her with her finances, all of the paperwork for the funeral and burial, and the house and the bills. I took her to her doctor's appointments and did the grocery shopping for her. Even though she had bent over backward to cater to her daughter, my mother, I cared for her when she couldn't care for herself. Mother was rarely there.

While all of this was going on, I was training to run my first ever marathon! I had always been a runner and it had gotten to the point that being out running was, somehow therapeutic to me. I would feel amazing after long runs and being that I had competed at anything in a while, my friend Lisa and I decided to run at the San Diego Marathon.

Chad was okay with it when I first mentioned it, but he thought it was something I said I would do but wasn't serious about. Then, as I stopped going drinking so I would wake up early to run, he started to resent that I wanted to do it. He'd say little comments but we never got into a full-on argument about it.

My sister, Lisa, Anas, and I flew out to San Diego the night before the race. I was nervous but felt I had prepared enough to at least finish it. Sis and Anas came for moral and emotional support. Chad wasn't happy about it and he let me know it.

He called me and was yelling at me for not being home. In his mind, I had left him for a stupid marathon. I tried calming him down, telling him I was going to be back the following day, but his anger had gotten to the point when he couldn't or wouldn't listen to the other person.

"How could you leave me?" He repeated. "I don't see why you have to be running it. Why can't you find an interest in things I'm interested in? How selfish can you be?"

I tried to tell him it wasn't like I was in Vegas with single girl-friends looking to party. "I'll be in bed early tonight to run tomorrow. I don't know what you're so mad about."

"I've told you over and over again what I'm upset about. How stupid can you be to not know? Do you even listen to me?!"

The worst part of it all was that I thought he had called to wish me luck so I answered the call in front of my sister. Although she didn't hear everything he said, and I tried to not let it show how angry he was, she knew exactly the type of support he was giving me.

The next morning I ran my first, and last, marathon. It was exciting at first, then after a few miles it got really real. It took everything I had in me but I finished it – without my boyfriend's support. I came home expecting an argument but he welcomed me back with open arms, a kiss, and a smile. I had no idea how to figure him out but he was Prince Charming again.

He knew I didn't like attention. But since I knew he loved attention, I had told him that if he were ever to propose, not to make a big spectacle of it. So, one evening, alone at our apartment, he got down on one knee, said some nice things to me, revealed an engagement ring, and asked me to marry him. I quickly said yes and kissed and hugged him. Then, he took the ring and put it on my finger. I was ecstatic! The ring was super pretty; it was simple and elegant, like me.

CHAPTER SEVEN
A WEDDING, A DEATH. A LIFE

Prior to our wedding, Chad quit his job, went to the city, and created his company, Carter Contractors. At first, I was skeptical that he was doing the right thing, but he reassured me that he had an "in" – a friend of his worked for an insurance company and agreed to give Chad the leads for all the claims he worked on. "So, they get the money from the insurance company; it doesn't cost them anything, and I'll do the work."

"How do you know you'll get the job?" I asked.

Chad smiled. "Come on. Look at me." He flexed his muscles and raised his jaw slightly; "There isn't anyone around as charismatic and charming as your future husband. I'm the best salesman around." He said it with a playful smile, and I laughed, even though we both knew he believed what he said one hundred percent.

Whether he was full of himself or not, the man told the truth. He quickly started to make much more money. I also made a career change and began to bring in much more money than before. We were able to buy a lot and started getting our first house built.

As I mentioned, I'm a simple Texan who never liked getting too much attention, so Chad and I decided on a small destination wedding. I found a great company in Cancun, Mexico, owned and

31

operated by two American girls, and hired them to set up every aspect of the wedding. They did a great job finding the perfect beach location, the flowers, the licenses (paperwork), the rooms for our guests, the cake, the photographers, and the female pastor – all of it for one price!

Around this time, I met my mother-in-law in person for the first time. Chad talked a lot about his mother and how great she was, what a great relationship they had, and how much I was going to love her. "If someone doesn't like my mom, something is wrong with them!"

Well, I didn't like her. I tried! But she wasn't very friendly towards me! She wasn't mean, just not... warm. I did my best and gave her my best Southern smile and hospitality, but she never reci-procated. If I had to make excuses for her, I could mention that she grew up in a military family and moved a lot when she was growing up, so she never had close friends, or maybe it was because I (a stranger to her) was taking her son away from her (I doubt she was like that with his first wife, or then again, maybe she's the reason they didn't last long!). Or, I can say how she was married to a Game Warden in Oklahoma and then became a traveling nurse, working in Colorado, Alaska, and other places for three months at a time – no doubt the sign of a marriage in trouble. (They would divorce and she moved to Fort Worth to be closer to her son – and me!).

The big day arrived: January 12, 2002. Our wedding was beau-tiful, picturesque even. The beach was perfectly calm, both the water and the wind. The white chairs were lined up perfectly. I walked barefoot onto the beach when my music played. I had the dress of my dreams, complete with a thin, elegant veil. We said our vows, he kissed his blushing bride, and everyone applauded. Love, joy, and hope were in the air.

It was a small, quaint wedding, with no more than 20 people who made the trip. We hung out with family and close friends, such as my mother, grandmother, my sister and her husband, Stacie, Kathy and her husband, Alesha, Paula, and other friends. The only one who made it from Chad's side was his mother. The hotel was all-inclusive, so we partied with them until they left a few days later.

Chad and I stayed a few more days and did all the touristy things like visiting the island, eating where locals ate, snorkeling, and buying anything that had Cancun printed on it.

I was super happy. We were married! My other relationships ended because we couldn't get on the same page regarding marriage. Then, I met an incredible, outgoing, good-looking, good-talking man, and he was dying to marry me. We arrived home and saw that the construction had begun at our single-story, three-bedroom, two-bath house north of Frisco. The future was bright.

We talked more seriously about having children. In the fall, we decided it was time to try to have children, so I stopped taking birth control. I got pregnant the month after. I was ecstatic! Chad and I started having an amazing marriage, we were building a house, and I was expecting our first child! I was beaming. However, it was short-lived because I had a miscarriage ten weeks later. To say I was devastated would be an understatement. I cried myself to sleep many nights. I had an inner battle in my mind; I almost had every-thing I wanted... *what if I could never have kids?*

However, God was gracious, and a month later, I got pregnant again. We found out it would be a boy. Soon, Cooper Carter would make his appearance on this planet. Life was amazing!

Long before any of this, my grandmother had started to have heart problems. She was rushed to the hospital a couple of times, but both times, the doctors said it was gas and there was nothing they could do, so they sent her back home, both times. At this time, when my life was totally amazing, she felt like she was having heart problems again. She called for an ambulance, and it still hurts my heart when I think of it; my grandmother died of a heart attack on the way to the hospital.

I took solace in the fact that she was able to see me get married and knew I was pregnant with Cooper. She told me many times, in her later days that she was proud of me and how much she loved me. Her funeral was incredibly hard for me. Other than arthritis, she was very active and healthy, so her death came as a shock. She had made me the executor of her will, and pregnant and all, I had the duties of overseeing the disbursements of her assets to my mother and uncle.

Being pregnant, I had stopped hanging out at bars, although it didn't stop Chad. I didn't mind. He was working very hard and was starting to bring in the type of money he told me he could. I was proud of him. I was more than content to sit at home, belly in hand, talking to Belly-Cooper, while his father was letting out steam from the pressures he put himself under.

It was three weeks before my due date when I said to Chad, "Either my water broke or I just peed on myself!"

The doctor reassured us we had time, so I took a shower, gathered whatever I would need, and Chad drove us to the Presbyterian Hospital in Dallas in the middle of the night. I was encouraged to have an epidural, even though I told the doctor I was thinking of going natural since I had a high pain tolerance. The pain of labor was very intense, even with the epidural. Chad, my mother, and my sister were all in and out of the room for the twelve hours of labor. Finally, Cooper decided it was time to make his grand entrance. It was a magical moment for all of us.

Chad was there that evening and held his son, his face beaming joyfully. However, he got up early in the morning and went to work. "I have another mouth to feed," he smiled as he left the room.

I was dancing on the inside, yet my body was in pain as I brought Cooper home. My mother-in-law, a labor and delivery nurse, insisted she stay with us for the first week. I thought it was a long time for someone unpleasant to you to stay in your house while your husband was at work or the bar. But, to my delight, she knew a lot about newborns and was very helpful with Cooper, although she was still very matter-of-fact with me.

I'd heard it said many times, but I never realized the weight of the words until my mother-in-law left, and it was just Cooper and I. Babies don't come with manuals! Like most moms, I had to figure it out for myself. I tried breastfeeding for four weeks, but he wasn't getting enough milk. Besides, it was very painful for me. I even got a breast infection and had to put a head of cabbage on my breasts to relieve the infection. After a month of pain and sadness that I couldn't physically feed my son, I decided to give him formula.

Cooper became my world. I was on his time schedule. When he woke up at night, I woke up – Chad had made it clear that he was the provider and I had to take care of the baby and the house, which was fine with me. I'm a traditional southern girl, and I would not have had it any other way, other than maybe having him take Cooper for a few hours so I could nap or bathe. But this is the life I had wanted and was grateful for having it.

Chad has a half-younger brother, Brian – they had the same father but different mothers. Sadly, Brian, who was 19 at the time, had drug issues and needed a place to stay. Chad offered him our extra room only if he would go to work for him and learn a trade. Brian lived with us for six months, and kudos to him; he kicked the drug habit, learned a trade, moved back to Oklahoma, and started his own flooring company. However, what sticks out most in my memories of Brian's time with us are the many times Chad would yell at him to clean his room, stop sleeping in, and stop playing video games. As for me, Brian was a nice, respectful kid and we got along great.

A baby in the house is a game changer. The house hears when he or she cries. Even though they don't speak words, their messages are conveyed and need to be met with urgency, or it will be a long, long night. Having experienced it firsthand, Chad and I talked a lot about having other kids. Ultimately, we decided Cooper needed a sibling, and we would love another child; however, if we were to do it, we needed to do it soon so they wouldn't be too far apart in age. I was on birth control, but we agreed I'd get off it and see if God would grace us with another child. A month later, I was pregnant with another boy, Cole, who was forming into the baby he would be to enter the world. We were ecstatic! Two boys! Or, as I thought of it, two Momma's Boys!

I had gone back to work while doing the accounting duties for Chad's company and still working part time at my office job. I would bring Cooper to the office with me. He would stay in a play pen while I worked.

35

Cole came to us in January of 2006. Our family was complete.

That part of my life was incredible. I'm very grateful for those years and many that followed. The only thing that perturbed me during that time was when I was driving with Cooper secured in the back seat and my mother-in-law in the front seat. In conversation, I mentioned to her that Chad and I had agreed that we would only have two kids, and once Cole was born, I'd have the doctors tie my tubes. My mother-in-law responded, "Well, that's a good thing. If you ever get remarried, you won't have to worry about having more kids."

Her words played over and over in my head. Why would a mother-in-law say that to the woman who is madly in love with and married to and gave birth to two sons to your son? Why would she mention a future with her son and me not being together?

I would find out later how unfaithful Chad had been and would realize that, at that point in time, she already knew it.

Mothers-in-law... am I right? SMH…

CHAPTER EIGHT
HERE COMES THE MONEY!

Carter Contractors hit the market with a bang. We didn't have the money to buy our first investment property, but Chad convinced his mother, my brother-in-law and others to lend him the money. True to his word, he paid every penny back with the agreed-upon interest. It was never a problem again for him to raise capital or find a lender to buy a house. He would look for older homes and do three things: buy them, fix them, and sell them. Then, as he gained experience and contacts in the industry, he started working exclusively with one realtor who found before-market homes (homes for sale that haven't been listed on the MLS or made public), fixed them, and resold them at a much higher price than what he bought them for.

"We only need to do three things to make a ton of money," He would tell his employees and me, "One, find the right property. Two, have the know-how to fix them quickly and with attention to detail. Three, put it on the market for a fair price. If we consistently do those three things, we'll dominate the market.

Chad was truly blessed in his understanding of real estate. He would get loans with a high interest rate, but it wouldn't matter because the interest was paid on the settlement statement when we bought the house, so he would never use our own money if he could flip it within 90 days, which he did the majority of the time.

He got to know all of the real estate investors in the area, all wealthy people looking at how to make passive income. They would pool their money to buy an asset with an undeniable return on investment (ROI), he and his team would fix and flip the house, everyone would get paid out, and they would do it again and again and again.

He quickly became known as the guy who would buy houses in cash, even if they didn't pass inspection. (Houses that didn't pass inspection are much harder to sell). He started using a hard money lender so he could buy as many houses as he found that fit his criteria. He used the same hard money lender for the first 13 years.

The money started pouring in. Between 2007 and 2008, he closed on a hunting ranch. It boasted a 3-bedroom, 2-bathroom house on 360 acres with fresh ponds and plenty of deer that he would lure in with deer feeders so he could hunt them. He also bought some ATVs (All-Terrain Vehicles), and he and some of his friends would go four-wheeling and hunting on weekends. The kids and I would go sometimes, but he went much more than we did alone.

He bought the boat he wanted, and we kept it at a nearby marina. When he didn't want to go the ranch, we – his wife and kids, or his friends would go boating on weekends. I never decided which one we did or which he did by himself. It was the Chad Carter show, and I was just a guest.

As a married couple, we got into a groove that, perhaps, many wouldn't think of as healthy, yet it worked well enough for us. He would work hard and play hard, and I would take care of the kids and manage the company's finances, which were growing monthly. At times, he would come home at 4 in the morning, and we'd argue because the bar he said he was at would close at 2 in the morning, but he would find a way to turn it on me. "I'm doing everything a husband is supposed to do. Don't nag me if I don't come home exactly when you expect me to. Everything is fine. This is normal for people with money like us. I make sure to provide you with all the comforts you can imagine. Can't I come to my house and have peace?"

I was so involved with the kids, with their health, finding the perfect schools, and the challenges of ensuring our finances were in order, that I let him do whatever he wanted without much "nagging." Regardless of his nighttime arrivals, he made sure we were always intimate. He felt that because he was such a great provider, my duty was to be intimate with him whenever he felt the urge. He was ready when he was ready, whether I wanted to or not.

Still, that didn't stop him from frequenting strip bars alone or with his friends, no doubt being – The Man – spending thousands of dollars a night. Thousands of dollars a night!

Sure, I would question and sometimes fight with him when he came home much later than the club closed, reeking of cheap perfume. He would tell me, "Relax. You know I'm a hugger. It's not like I'm having sex with them or anything." Sometimes, when I'd be really mad, he'd use the kids for us not to fight. "It's always the same with you! Look, I'm drunk, and you're about to piss me off. You know how I get. Don't make me yell and wake up the kids. No one wants that, especially you."

Even though he'd be rude to me occasionally, we did get along, even though we didn't spend much time together. In 2006, he bought me a Mercedes CLS 500 (4-door). He bought me a G500 Black Mercedes (G-Wagon) in 2008. In 2009, 7 years after our marriage, he bought me a new wedding ring – a 4-karat beauty that looked a little out of place on my tiny finger.

As you read this, you may think that my husband might have been a partier, but he sure did love me by giving me all those gifts, but you'd be wrong. It became clear to me that he gave me the cars and ring to show people he could afford it. I'd hear him talking/bragging on the phone about what he bought me. Also, I understand that people try to buy you in some ways in exchange for their absence. Even though I was also working for the company doing its books, he always reminded me that he bought them for me. "I don't know why you ever complain," he'd say, "you're the envy of all women, and it still isn't enough!" I sometimes yelled back, "I haven't asked for any of this! I'd rather live a simpler life with a more present husband!"

I'm a natural nurturer and looked into nursing school, but he said he didn't want me to return to work. Then, he listed reasons why I wouldn't like it anyway. Ultimately, he felt I should have thanked him for enlightening me about myself and saving me the arduous journey to become a nurse and the job I would have. At the end of the day, I believe now that he never wanted me to make my own money for fear that I might leave him since that was just about all he brought to the relationship.

"But I can tell you're antsy; let's go on a vacation, just me and you. Besides, I need a deep-sea fishing fix." He took us to Costa Rica and had a fabulous time. We did some deep-sea fishing, spent time gambling at the casino, went to a few beaches, and zip-lined throughout the country. It's still one of the best places I've ever visited. We would also go to Cancun with the kids and the Bahamas a few times when his mother moved there for a short time. Even though we went on some luxurious vacations, Chad would mostly be working or partying, even during the holidays.

I didn't have an idle, boring life. I was a hands-on, full-time mother. I was going to birthdays, practices, games, doctor's appointments, playdates, etc. I managed the finances for the business, which were mind-blowing. I also managed our personal finances, which were also mind-blowing. We had some years when we would gross between $20 million to $30 million yearly. Even though Chad and I stayed intimate, I felt emptiness. That is, until I met Billy.

Billy was a very successful attorney; his kids went to the same preschool as mine, so we would attend the same birthday parties. He would always tell me to feel free to contact him if I ever needed anything he could help with. Months later, I called him because Chad had gotten a speeding ticket, and he did a great job in making it go away.

We were both at a kid's party where they were serving alcohol. I was used to the cakes, balloons, and ice cream, but not the amount of alcohol available there. My phone pinged, and I saw a text from

Billy – he had my phone number from when he helped me with the ticket.

> I wonder how many DUI clients I will get from this KID's party!

The joke took me off guard, and I laughed out loud. I texted him back:

> If you charge double for every percent over the alcohol limit, you'd have enough to retire!

We continued to chat via text, every once in a while, seeing each other from across the room and smiling. I was always at functions without my husband. I would often see Billy at functions without his wife. We texted about funny/silly stuff for the rest of the day. I was surprised to find a text from him early the next morning. It felt nice that an adult was interested in conversing with me. While my days were busy, they were void of adult friendship. If Chad wasn't working, he'd be hunting with his friends or at the bar or strip joint. Billy, on the other hand, was a hands-on dad. It felt nice; warm even, to talk to a father who knew so much about his kids.

While he wasn't my type physically, I was attracted to the human being he was: a good father, a good provider, and, from what I knew, an overall good person. He wasn't a partier or known to spend time at bars.

We continued to text each other daily. He was never disrespectful, and we didn't cross any lines, but he would flirt with me occasionally. With the lack of any attention from another adult, I became emotionally dependent on his texts. I knew of his wife and wouldn't sleep with him or anyone's husband, no matter what, but it sure felt nice to know another man was thinking of me. But Billy wanted more.

He very badly wanted to meet me in person. After turning that notion down many times, I finally agreed, but with the stipulation that it had to be during the day and at a public place. I'm not the type to meet a guy in a corner for alcoholic drinks or anything. I agreed to meet him at a local Starbucks, and we sat there, drinking coffee with plenty of people around us. I wasn't nervous about meeting with him because I knew I would never do anything, and I never thought he'd step far out of line aside from more compliments. However, I was nervous that if Chad found out, he would flip. Maybe it was the boredom or the spontaneity, but I met Billy for coffee twice at the same Starbucks. We never as much as held hands, but I did enjoy his comedic personality. With Chad gone most weekends, I didn't think much of it.

During this time, Cooper had finished kindergarten in Celina, and we wanted him to go to a Christian private school so he would be pushed academically and be surrounded by students with similar interest. We also agreed that we wanted him to be indoctrinated to the bible through their curriculum. We found a great school in Frisco, which was a long drive for me to do daily. We moved to Frisco in 2010 to our first million-dollar home. It was, by far, the prettiest home I'd ever seen. Cinderella had found her castle.

Everything would have been great, except that Chad had found the texts between Billy and me, and he was pissed!

CHAPTER NINE

THE SEPARATION AND MY MOM

THE SEPARATION

While moving into the new house, Chad stormed in and told me to come to, what was to be, our new bedroom. He took a stack of papers from his briefcase and threw them on a dresser, the only piece of furniture in the room. I glanced at them and my stomach churned. He had every single text from Billy and me printed out, with parts of them highlighted.

He was livid. "Is this what you do when I'm not home? Is this how you repay me while I'm out there busting my ass for this family?"

He went on and on, hardly allowing me to say anything. "Meeting someone for coffee is nothing happening? Are you stupid? Look at these texts," he read some of them to me. "Can't you tell that he's hitting on you, or are you that stupid?"

I could have gone back at him for all of the late nights at strip joints and him coming home hours after it closed reeking of perfume, but I thought he would think I was having an affair and blame it on that. No matter what he said, I would not admit I had a sexual affair because it wasn't true.

43

I did apologize for hiding the text conversations from him, but he cut me off when I tried to tell him that I was just happy that anyone wanted to talk to me. He didn't listen to me. He was on a roll, playing the woe-is-me victim. "What if someone saw you? What would they think of me?"

"It's always about you!" I yelled.

The argument ended with him taking some clothes and moving into an already furnished apartment, which he had secured even before our argument. Before leaving, he called Billy from my phone and told him he knew all about our communication and that he better tell his wife or he would call his wife and let her know. He then deleted Billy's number from my phone. I never communicated with him again.

I was left alone to put the house in order with the kids and the movers. We still talked every day. One might think it was because I had the kids, but most of our conversations were about the company's finances because I was handling it even though I wasn't an accountant. Our relationship turned from a married couple to a client and his personal bookkeeper.

He dropped the bomb one day. "By the way, I think I should tell you, I'm seeing someone. Her name is Mercedes." I was devastated. It turned out that she worked in home warranties and Chad had dealings with her constantly, if not every day. He sighed and then said, "I want a divorce."

I was surprised more than anything. I had always suspected he was fooling around, but I didn't expect him to want to separate. I called my sister, who lived out of the country, for support. "Don't worry, sis," She told me. "Once he finds out how much he stands to lose, he'll change his mind."

Sure enough, he changed his tune once Chad realized I was entitled to half of everything we had and we would split the time with the boys. "Look. It was you meeting Billy that made me start seeing somebody. But I'm not about to let you walk away with half of what I worked so hard for. I stopped seeing Mercedes. I'm coming back home."

And that was that. He was coming back home. No apology for

having a sexual affair with someone that he worked with and that people knew about. No asking me if he could come back. He just said he was coming back home. As I always did, I took it. I figured that marriages go through tough times and that we would get through this. Besides, I wanted my kids to be raised by their father. *I would find out later that Mercedes was married and that her affair with Chad ended her marriage.*

We started attending a non-denominational Christian Church. We had two pastors who would alternate giving sermons every Sunday. I liked getting two different styles and perspectives; it kept the sermons fresh. Both pastors knew how to quote scripture, but unlike other pastors I've known, they also knew how to relate it to day-to-day experiences and situations. I also loved their worship team. It quickly became our home church and a refuge of sorts for me.

I liked the church so much that I started attending bible studies weekly. I also volunteered in their office once a week. I did whatever they needed, whether sending out mailers and welcome letters, being a part of the welcome team, or setting up activities – whatever. I was a volunteer on the Parent Teacher Organization board at the boy's school for eight years. The first three years I helped run the spirit shop, two years as the president and three years as the new family coordinator. There were some employees that would joke that I needed an office at the school since I was there so much.

We stayed in our new home for two years. Then, Chad, always looking for the next big thing, decided for us to buy a new house in 2012. It was a gorgeous $1.4 million home on 3 acres of land, a great pool, guest house and a huge pond in front of the house that the boys would fish from. I loved the house but didn't feel we needed one so big. However, Chad wanted it and it didn't matter what town we lived in since the boys were in private school. With all our moving, I wanted at least their school to have some continuity.

45

MOM

Right around the time we moved into the new house, my mother's heart condition started to worsen. She was living alone at my sister's house and was dependent on me to take her to her appointments, much like my grandmother did during the last stages of her life. Her doctor determined that she needed a heart transplant.

"There's good news and bad news, and good news," the doctor said. "The good news is that her frame is so small, and her heart is so small, she needs a child-sized heart – and those are much easier to find than an adult-sized heart."

"What's the bad news?" Mom asked.

"Well, those hearts only last roughly 15 years, so in that time, we'll have to find you another one. But then the good news is that you can wait to get it. We'll monitor you to ensure you get it when you need it."

"So, you're not putting her on the transplant list now?" I asked.

"Not at this time. Don't worry, Shelley, we've got plenty of time."

Months later, I told her doctor that she was running out of breath walking from the front door to the car and wasn't getting around much at all. They told me that was the sign they were waiting for and began the process of putting her on the transplant list. However, she needed to undergo a series of tests to get on the list. Unfortunately, her body wasn't ready for the tests and her lungs failed. She went from okay when she walked into the hospital to being on a ventilator. My sister didn't waste time and flew into the country to be with her.

Our mother passed away in the hospital in July of 2013.

I felt they waited a year too late to put her on the transplant list. Before going to the visit that would require her to stay there, I had set up for her to stay at our guest house and for my assistant Ashley, my sister, and I to provide the care she needed. She never ended up moving into the guest house. My sister and I were devastated.

My mother wasn't the perfect role model when I was growing up. She showed me more about what not to do and how not to act than what to do and behave appropriately. However, her life changed once she accepted the Lord as her personal savior. Her final years were spent sober, attending church, telling everyone about God, and loving on my kids. She would visit the boys several times each week. Cooper particularly looked forward to when she would take him on her "job" as a dog walker. It was the thing he most looked forward to.

If there's one thing I can say about God, it is that He changed my mother's life for the better, and I'm blessed to know she's with Him now.

CHAPTER TEN

TOM AND AGENT ROB

Even though I was mourning the death of my mother, time did what it always does: it kept going. Chad was also doing what he did; he kept bringing in and spending money. I wasn't surprised when he drove to the house in his brand-new H-1 Hummer. The thing was massive. "This is my weekend toy," he smiled. True enough, he would go to work in his F250, but as soon as Friday night came, whether he was staying in town or going away to his friend's lake house, he was in that Hummer. The man did not shy away from attention.

"Do you know what we need?" he asked me one day. I thought about it and couldn't guess what we possibly needed. In the bare sense of survival, we had all the necessary food, shelter, and transportation. Regarding luxury, the boys were in the best schools, we had homes, a big boat, luxury cars, bling that could blind someone, designer clothes, shoes, and bags.

"I honestly don't know if we actually *need* anything, Chad. But tell me, what are you going to buy next?"

"A dockominium," he stated. His eyes gleamed. "No one has one. Of course, they'll copy me once they see mine."

I sorta knew what it was but had to look it up just to be certain.

Sure enough, a dockominium is just what the words meshed together mean – it's a building (condominium) on the dock in a marina slip that's floating and secured. Chad hired people to build a 3-bedroom, 2-bath, 2-story, water-based home next to our boat slip. It was overkill but it was also pretty spectacular. Soon after, others in the marina started building them, just like Chad predicted.

Time kept moving on and the boys continued getting bigger and more involved in sports. Much of my time during the week was spent bringing them to and from their practices. During the weekends, Chad and I would attend their games, which meant, we didn't use the boat nearly as often as we once did. I got tired of driving to Frisco four to six times a week, so we moved back in 2014. We bought a $1.2 million home in a neighborhood. It had a pool but less land than our previous house. The boys were also a little upset they didn't have their own pond they could fish from, but they adjusted quickly once they jumped in the pool.

Chad went on a selling spree. He sold the boat, dockominium and the Hummer to the same person. He didn't want to sell the Hummer, but it didn't fit in the garage at the new house, even though it was a 3-car garage. We also sold all 8 of the rental properties we had.

Flush with an overabundance of cash but always wanting more, Chad decided to move on from focusing on homes. He began developing office strips – where doctors or dentists would have offices, and/or insurance companies. He bought some land in Frisco and went to the same lender he had always used to get the loan to start the project. I don't think Chad expected the learning curve to be as difficult as it was, being that he had never built anything like that, but he willed his way through it. He got excited once it was nearly done and wanted to build multiple strips at a time. However, the lender wasn't comfortable loaning that much money and told Chad they would fund one project at a time. Nothing frustrated Chad more than someone telling him he couldn't do something.

He voiced his frustrations to our friends. I would hear bits of the conversation. "Small minded....insecure....he'll never be great...

who does he think he is….this is my business…if he doesn't do it, someone else will…."

He gave the rant to Ron, a parent of one of the kids who attended our son's school. Ron was the president of a multi-million dollar company. If you're interested, I have a great lender." Ron said. "I'll give you his number. If it's a good deal, he'll jump on it." Chad met Tom in 2015 and it changed the trajectory of our lives forever.

He came home from meeting Tom full of enthusiasm. "I told you nothing can hold me back. Not only is he interested in working with me, but he's offering less interest than what I was getting! I think I found my guy."

"Chad," I countered calmly. He would get excited and forget the times he had made mistakes, and as his wife, I tried to make him slow down when I felt he was going too fast. "We've been with the same lender for 13 years. You've done amazing things with them. We don't know anything about this Tom guy. I think it's risky to jump into business of this magnitude with someone you just met."

"That's why you're not a business person, Shelley. Fortune favors the bold. The greater the risk, the bigger the payoff. You should trust me by now. I've proven that I know what I'm doing."

Ron, who referred Tom to Chad, had gone into business with one of the stay-at-home moms whose kid also went to the same school, Annie. Ron put up the money up and built an Emergency Room Care business. Annie had plenty of experience in that field and, it was her idea in the first place. Her role was to put in sweat equity by running the clinic. Ron had it built and sat back, waiting for the return on his investment. However, things went bad quickly. Ron accused Annie of mismanaging the money. Annie was adamant that she was doing what needed to be done for the business. They had a huge fallout, and Ron cut her out of the deal.

Annie was irate. It was her idea; now that it was up and running, she was left with nothing. One of her kids was on the same soccer team as a Homeland Security agent's son. They had become friends. So, Annie told the agent what had happened and, by his own volition, he decided to look into it.

The agent – Agent Rob – took a deep dive into Ron's professional finances. His search led him directly to Tom, his lender. Ron had to take out a loan from Tom once Annie was removed from the business in order to keep it running. He went to Tom's website and wrote down the companies listed on it – one was North 40, Chad's company.

In October, Agent Rob visited an acquaintance of ours, the Friedman's. I didn't know this at the time. What I did know was that all of a sudden, the Friedman's moved away. They were a very well-established and well-to-do family. Apparently, Agent Rob told him not to do business with Tom anymore and the Friedman's got spooked, sold everything, and move away.

Doing his due diligence, Agent Rob started looking at North 40's business dealings with Tom. I knew nothing about this until Agent Rob knocked on my door.

I was home wrapping presents on Christmas Eve when someone rang the doorbell. The kids were upstairs playing, so I got up and opened the door. A tall man dressed in slacks, a button shirt, and a coat smiled at me and waved a badge.

"Hello, ma'am. My name is Agent Rob. Is your husband Chad here, by chance?"

The man waived the badge so quickly that I couldn't read anything on it. I was taken aback and wasn't sure what to say. "Um, no, he's not. Can I help you with something?"

"Are you sure? I just have a couple of questions for him."

"Yes, I'm sure. He's probably at the office. Or, being that it's Christmas Eve, he might be shopping. "Can you call him on the phone now?" I'll see if I can get him on the line for you. I called Chad but he didn't answer. "Do you want to leave a card or something?"

He smiled. "No thanks. I'll get in touch with him next year. Enjoy the Holidays."

Chad called me back not too long after Agent Rob drove out of the driveway. "Some badge-flipper came here asking for you."

"Badge-flipper?" He laughed. "What about?"

"He didn't say."

"What agency was he with?"

"He flipped it so fast I couldn't tell. I asked if he wanted to leave a card but he said no."

"Well, then, it's nothing to worry about. Oh, I might be home a little late tonight."

"It's Christmas Eve," I said.

"That's why I'm spending time with some of my employees. I'll be with you and the boys all day on Christmas Day. Don't wait up."

A few weeks later, Agent Rob visited Chad in his office. Chad came home upset. "The nerve of that guy!"

"Who?"

"The stupid badge-flipper with the cheap shoes. He came to my office today to tell me he's doing an investigation, and that Tom is under suspicion of something. Whatever it is, he said he couldn't tell me."

"Who's he with?" I asked.

"Get this. Homeland Security! What the hell is Homeland Security doing investigating a lending company? He said he was looking into something. I bet he's not even supposed to be investigating whoever he's investigating. This guy is way out of line. I should report him."

"What did he actually say?"

"He told me that I should stop doing business with Tom."

"If someone from Homeland Security is telling you not to do business with Tom, maybe you shouldn't."

Chad scoffed, "Do you know how much money Tom stands to make me through the different deals we're working on? Of course you don't!"

I was used to Chad getting angry and finding a way to blame me, so I kept the conversation on track. I wanted to tell him I warned him about Tom but he would have flipped out on me. "What are you going to do?"

"I told him neither one of us are doing anything wrong. I told him, 'Thanks for your concern, but no thanks,' and had him leave my office. Nobody tells me who I can or can't do business with."

I adjusted my shirt, knowing he wanted to get more off of his chest but not wanting to say anything that would turn his anger on me. "The nerve of that guy!" He yelled. "He came to my house, MY HOUSE, on Christmas Eve? He knew my number and where my office was, why would he come to my house to talk to my wife? I'm sure you don't know why so I'll tell you. To scare you and to intimidate me. But you know what? I'm not falling for that bullshit. I do whatever the hell I want."

In the weeks that followed, I told Chad that everyone knew Tom was under investigation and it wasn't a good look for us to be doing business with him. However, he told me for the millionth time that I knew nothing about business. "Just take care of the kids and let me take care of the business. You decide what they eat for lunch, I decide what we do and how we make money."

Six months later, they raided Tom's office and shut him down.

CHAPTER ELEVEN
INDICTED

"You're not going to believe this crap!" Chad said as he stormed into the house. I was in another room but quickly went to the foyer where he was. He walked by me and headed straight to the master bedroom. "This country is going crazy."

He put away the rolling bag he took with him everywhere; it was a cross between a briefcase and a luggage because it had wheels and he'd drag it behind him everywhere because he had all of his important papers in there. He motioned for me to put my phone away and go with him to the walk-in closet. He always felt our phones were being tapped, even when they weren't in use. He handed me his phone and I set them both in the bathroom, shut the door and went into the closet.

"Can you tell me what's going on?" I asked. For an instant, I thought he would yell at me; maybe that something was my fault or I wouldn't understand – like he often did.

"This Agent Rob is a piece of work. You know how he, all by himself and under no direction from his higher-ups, was investigating Tom?" I nodded. "Well, he found something, but since he's a small-time government employee with no real pull, he brought in the Texas Securities Board, and they raided Tom's office!" I let out a soft gasp. I wanted to tell Chad I had told him not to get into business with Tom, but Chad was so worked up that I thought it would be better to let him tell me everything first.

"The Texas Securities Board?" I had never heard of that organization.

"Yes, Shelley, The Texas Securities Board. There are regulations for everything, including securities – supposedly, this board protects investors. They had sent Tom a Cease and Desist Letter, but we knew he wasn't doing anything wrong, so he kept getting me my loans. They took his computer and all of his paperwork. It's becoming that once you get successful, one agency or other will try to bring you back down."

"Did they find anything?" I asked.

"How the hell would I know!" Chad yelled. "This just happened! I'm sure they're going to owe him a huge apology afterward, but in the meantime, I get screwed over because I don't have the money to pay back the investors until the projects are completed!"

I didn't know how much into the millions Chad's projects added to, but he was working on four major, multi-million dollar projects and needed more funds to pay for them to get finished. He was beyond irritated and was full-on pissed off. I tiptoed around him and reminded him that the boys could hear what he said, but to little avail. When Chad was mad, he wanted everyone to know it.

"This Texas Securities Board is on a rampage. A few months earlier, they arrested a guy named Jim, who Tom was lending money to. Get this. Jim is a pastor. They're arresting pastors now! What in the world is going on?"

After about a week of him grumbling about how he would get the money, he came home whistling and kissed me on the cheek when he walked in.

"What's the reason for this sudden burst of happiness?" I asked with a smile.

"I found the work-around. There's a guy who worked for Tom, whose name is Scott. He actually did all the work for Tom on my projects. I had lunch with him today, and he will continue doing what he did for me through Tom."

"And what did he do for you?" I asked. I was far past asking what someone did for us regarding money or the company. It was all what they did for Chad.

"He got me the loans and investors."

"But honey, don't you think maybe you should work with another lender until this thing with Tom gets cleared?"

"Do you have any idea how long that would take? People need to get paid for their work now. Come on, Shelley. Think, for once."

"I am thinking, Chad, and it doesn't feel right."

"Well, you're wrong again. I hired an attorney and told him what was going on. He told me how to legally get the capital to pay investors back from the original lenders. As long as I get the capital to make the investors whole, I'm not doing anything illegal."

So, Chad started working with Scott, who worked for Tom, the same way he worked with Tom, who was out on bond awaiting a trial. There was no talking him out of it. Whenever I said anything, I was either ignored or insulted. One night, while he spoke about what his attorney said, I asked him if I needed an attorney.

"You? Why would you need one? You didn't talk to investors, you've never worked in the office, you've never met with the lender. All you do is stay home, pay bills, handle the kids, and spend my money."

He was right. All I did for the company was answer an email from him or one of his employees and send the exact amount of money they told me to the people or companies they told me. I wasn't involved in the planning or day-to-day operations. I was never at a staff meeting. So, I didn't hire an attorney. I figured if anyone were to investigate me, they would clearly see the minimal role I played.

Scott got more loans, and the money started coming in again. Chad was able to pay the different construction companies so they could stay on track. Building those office condos took a ton of money on the front end and during the building phase. We're not talking about a basic home with walls and windows; they were building commercial properties and needed permits, electricians, plumbers, designers, and much more. However, when it was done and sold, everyone involved walked away with substantial profits.

It turned out that Pastor Jim had started an online marketing company, and he used Tom to get huge loans. Apparently, his company brought in millions of dollars. However, Pastor Jim did not use the money the way he told his investors he would. Instead, he bought himself a beautiful home, luxury cars, and the finer things in life. He pled innocent and went to trial in May of 2018. Today, Pastor Jim is in a state prison, serving a 68-year sentence! He is going to die in jail for lying to people out of millions of dollars.

Tom's case was different. He got charged with selling securities without a license. I was floored when I heard the charge. He clearly knew he needed a license to get the loans. It turned out that Tom's daughter had gotten her securities license but didn't use it.

"How did you not know Tom didn't have a license?" I asked Chad.

"Get off my back! Every time I go into his office, I have these massive projects to think about. I saw a license hanging on the wall in Tom's office. The font they used, with weird cursive, was challenging to read. What sucks is that Tom knows how to do that job better than most who get a license!"

I must say, I was impressed by the gall Tom had. That man ran local radio ads on many AM stations to get investors. With him blatantly promoting himself the way he did, no one would question whether he had a license.

It never dawned on Chad that he and Scott were now doing – raising capital – the same way Tom was doing it – without a license! When I'd mention it to Chad, he'd remind me that I'm not a lawyer and that his very high-priced attorney told him he was fine.

"My attorney called the actual federal agent that sent me the target letter letting us know we were under investigation. He told the agent that I needed to get the money to pay everyone back. That agent told my attorney that as long as that was what I was doing, they had no reason to go after me. So, please, I have enough stress without coming home and having you stress me out."

"Well, hell, Chad, you probably should have told me that a long time ago! I'm over here worrying and praying for us, and you tell me this now?" I yelled as I stormed out of the room.

Tom was told the state would give him a plea bargain if he pled guilty. It turned out that his daughter, the one with the license, was his bookkeeper and far more involved in his business than I was in Chads's. Tom negotiated a plea deal and pled guilty, with the stipulation that his daughter would not be charged. The judge gave him 12 years.

An indictment was filed against Chad and me on November 8, 2018.

Five days later, November 13, 2018, they came to arrest us. I was beyond shocked.

CHAPTER TWELVE
ARRESTED

November 13, 2018, began like every other weekday. It was a brisk Tuesday morning, and I had my day planned out. I had laid out the boys' clothes the night before to make things easier for them and me in the morning. I woke up at six and helped get Cole ready for football practice at seven. I had to bring the dogs with us because after dropping him off, I had to scoot to the Vet clinic to get them groomed. I then had to return home, wake Cooper up, and take him to school.

I left the house in my pajamas, with Cole and the dogs in tow. I made great time, dropped him off at the football field early, and headed to the vet clinic. I brought the dogs in and got them situated before I ran out to wake Cooper up. That's when the day took an awful turn.

I pulled out of the parking lot and immediately got pulled over by an unmarked police vehicle. It was odd because I hadn't run a stop sign and just got out of a parking lot, so I couldn't have been speeding. "I hope this doesn't take a long time," I muttered as the officers in the unmarked car took their time getting out. They finally approached me and tapped on my window, which I opened halfway – not to be rude, but because it was a chilly November morning.

"Is your name Shelley Carter?" The officer nearest to me asked.

"Yes, sir, I am." I couldn't help but notice my Southern Texas accent as I said that. I thought I sounded just like Dolly Parton.

"Can we see some I.D.?

"Sure. But can you tell me why you're pulling me over?"

"Not right now, let's see that I.D. please, ma'am."

I fished my license out of my purse, grateful I had brought it. I probably would have left it if I weren't bringing the dogs to the vet. I handed it to the officer, and they stepped away from the window, which I instantly shut to stop the cold wind from coming in. I was in my pajamas!

The knock on the window startled me, and I lowered the window again. "Miss Carter, I'm going to have to ask you to step out of the vehicle." The same officer said.

"For what? It's cold out."

"Ma'am, I'm asking you to step out of the vehicle. Are you going to comply?"

I got out, and the other officer took me by my right elbow and turned me into my car. "Please turn around and put your hands behind your back. You're being arrested."

My mind went numb. "For what?"

"We can't tell you now, but you'll know soon enough."

"Don't tell me you're going to put me in the back of the car. I'm not a criminal."

They sat me in the front passenger seat with my hands hand-cuffed behind my back. One of the officers was communicating with someone else through the radio. I wasn't paying much attention because of the pain in my wrists from how tight the cuffs were, made worse because of my weight on them.

"Ma'am, to the best of your knowledge, is Mr. Chad Carter at home?"

"I guess so. I mean, he was sleeping when I left. If he's not at the house, he's at his office."

"If he were to be at home, where in the house would he be?" The officer asked me.

"What do you mean, where would he be? Probably the bedroom or master bathroom taking a shower, I'd imagine."

"Is that the upper front of the house or the back left of the house...?"

"Oh, the master is on the bottom floor, back left." That was the first time I had to give someone such specific locations for the interior of a home.

"Thank you," the officer got back on his radio but I interrupted him.

"Officer, we're good people. I have a son at home, and I have no idea what you all are planning on doing and how you plan on getting into my house. Can I please call my neighbor to wake up my son and get him out before you do what you're going to do?"

"Sorry, ma'am, we can't do that."

I'm not an easy crier, nor am I quick to get hysterical, but the thought of armed men breaking through my front door and slamming Cooper's bedroom door open, and shoving him to the ground with guns pointed at his face was enough for me to beg. "If you have children, you have to understand. You can still arrest my husband without giving our son serious trauma."

My pleas fell on deaf ears, or at least on ears that didn't have the authority to allow that to happen. I found out later that they knocked on the door, and no one answered. The dogs were getting groomed, so they weren't there to alert anyone that someone was outside the house.

As I suspected, Chad was in the shower. He told me later that he put a towel around him because he heard some commotion going on outside the house. He looked out the windows of the hallway and saw police officers with tactical gear and AK47s all around the house. He told me he grabbed one of his guns with the red laser and pointed it at the officers, and they pointed their guns at him. (I'm still unsure if that was true, but that's what he told me).

They busted through the back door and searched the entire house. They went to Cooper's room, who was still sleeping. He woke up to officers in full riot gear. They brought him downstairs, and he saw his father standing in the middle of the room in handcuffs.

They had let Chad get dressed, but he didn't have any shoes on, so one of the officers escorted Cooper into his father's closet, and Cooper picked out a pair of slides for him.

The officers with Chad seemed to have more authority than the ones who arrested me because they allowed Chad to call one of his employees to hurry to the house and pick up Cooper. Thankfully, he didn't live far and they waited for him – it was either that or they were going to call Child Protective Services.

In the meantime, I was still parked, sitting in the front seat of the unmarked vehicle as we all waited for a tow truck to get my car. It took them a little more than an hour. The handcuffs were now biting into my skin, but I didn't complain because I knew they wouldn't do anything about it. I had a feeling that because I had a G-Wagon, they probably thought I was some rich, spoiled brat.

Once the car got towed, we started to move. "Ma'am, get comfortable. Being that the charge originated from Collin County which had a warrant out for my arrest, that's where we need to take you. Maybe another twenty minutes."

Whether they thought I was a brat or not, the handcuffs hurt, so I asked again if they could loosen them. They said they couldn't but that they'd re-cuff me with my hands in front when we arrived.

"Can you tell me what I'm being arrested for now?" I asked.

"Money laundering."

My mind went in different directions. *There has to be some mistake. I pay the bills, but we're not laundering money. I wouldn't even know how to go about doing that!*

We finally arrived, and they parked in an indoor parking lot. True to their word, one of the officers un-cuffed me, allowed me to massage my wrists, and then re-cuffed me with my hands in front of me. It still hurt my wrists, but not nearly as much. I thanked them as they walked me into the booking station.

The arresting officer gave someone my purse and they thoroughly went through it, inventorying everything I had in it. Then, they took me for my "mug shot." I was numb to what was happening; I stared into the camera without a facial expression.

I have always been a rule follower. I won't even talk to people that talk about doing illegal things. Part of why I was like that was because I thought I would be so scared if I were ever to get arrested. However, I wasn't afraid at all. I was confused. Chad had told me that his attorney had said to him that if they were ever to arrest him, they would call his attorney, and he would tell him to turn himself in to the authorities. Then he'll walk into the jail with him, go through processing, and he'd be out in a few hours. Obviously, that did not happen. Somehow I was roped into this misunderstanding.

After my mug shot, I was brought to a large room-like lobby where males and females who were processed stayed. It had two rows of about 20 chairs in each row – each facing the wall, or better put, facing opposite of the other sex. I was explicitly told not to make eye contact with any men, including my husband. "No eye contact, hand signals, or movement of the eyebrows. No verbal or non-verbal communication at all. Got it?"

There were plenty of empty chairs, especially in the ladies section, so I was free to pick one of the empty plastic chairs and wait for them to call me. I looked at the clock on the wall and saw it was 8:30. I had been in "custody" since 7:15. The day was going slow, and now, sitting there with no phone and nothing to look at, it looked like it would go even slower.

The sound of new officers bringing someone in caught my attention. I glanced to the doorway and saw Chad handcuffed and flanked by two officers. His eyes bulged when he saw me. I noticed he was trying to mouth something to me, but I quickly looked away. Like I said, I am a rule follower and wanted to avoid getting into more trouble than I was already.

"Shelley Carter!" An officer called. I quickly got up and went over to him. "You can make a call, but then we need to change your clothes."

I had been thinking about who I would call, but the problem was I didn't know anyone's number. "Sir, is there any way I can get my phone so that I can call the appropriate people?"

The officer smirked, "I don't know anyone's number either. Hold tight."

I told him who I needed to call, and he went into my phone and got me the phone numbers. I called Ashley first. My sister was out of the country, and Ashley was my part-time assistant. She was in shock to get a call from me from jail. "I know. Me too. But listen, I don't think I'll get out of here before the boys get out of school. You are the only person on the list besides me who can pick them up."

"Ya, of course. I'll be there. What do you want me to tell them?"

"Well, Cooper knows what happened, but not Cole. If they ask, tell them we got caught up with work and we'll be home after dinner time."

My second call was to Chads's attorney's office. I was assured that we would be out soon. As we spoke, someone was putting up the bail money for us with a bail bondsman, which was 10% of the total bail. They paid $1,800 for me, meaning my bail was $18,000, and $3,500 for Chad, who had a $35,000 bond.

Then, a female cop took me to a changing room and made me change from my comfy pajamas to blue scrub-like clothes. She watched me the entire time.

I was told to go back to my seat and, when I did, sat next to some younger girls that were there. We couldn't communicate with the men, but the ladies could talk to each other. One girl was there for unpaid traffic tickets that turned into a warrant, and another girl was caught on a routine stop, but they had searched everyone and found a small amount of weed on her. I figured any conversation was better than sitting there doing nothing. However, I felt dirty and knew I would take a nice, long, hot shower when I returned home. Time continued to tick by. Some people that got there before me were leaving before me.

I'm usually not one to complain, but I went to the front desk several times. "My lawyer said they already paid the money. When do you think I'll be able to get leave?"

My questions were answered with rudeness. "I don't have time to talk to you. We'll call you when you can leave. Go sit back down."

I sat back down and waited for what felt like five hours. Then I heard, "Shelley Carter!" I got up and quickly walked to the officer who called me. "Come on, we need to get your fingerprints."

Before I knew it, I was back on a plastic chair by myself. The two younger girls had been released. I kept looking at the big clock, wondering what would happen if I was still there at five PM. I didn't bother asking the rude people at the desk, so I just sat there, worrying. At around five, they took me to a nurse's area. They had me do a U.A. to make sure I wasn't pregnant.

"I had my tubes tied. We don't have to do this. I can't be pregnant." I informed the nurse.

"Do you know how many people lie to us about the silliest things? I believe you had your tubes tied, but we still need to go through the process. The same woman who watched me change entered the bathroom with me and watched me pee into the cup. It was humiliating. It turned out I wasn't pregnant. I wasn't surprised.

At around 5 PM, they brought me into the nurse's area for a tuberculosis shot. "Wait. Why am I getting a tuberculosis shot?"

"It's for your own protection for once you get to the jail." A female guard answered, the same one that watched me pee."

"My bond was posted this morning. I'm not staying in jail. I am not taking that shot." I said. The guard said well if you refuse the shot then you will be held in solitary confinement. She sat me down in a chair outside the nurse's station. I heard Chad's name being called to be released out on bail. He had gotten there later than me but was leaving before me. I thought about going to the desk to see what the hold-up was, but I knew they would just tell me to sit down, so I just sat down.

"Shelley Carter?" the female cop called, like she didn't know who I was at that point. "You're being released." I was so relieved because they were about to take me to get a TB shot or solitary confinement.

I was led to where I got my stuff back and told I was free to leave. I turned on my phone and got the text that Chad was outside waiting. When I walked out, he was there with Kelly, who had picked up Cooper, and Chad's assistant, Suzy whom Kelly was dating.

"What's going on with the kids?" I asked Chad. I knew we had to talk about the day's events, but my mind was on my boys.

"Cooper ended up not going to school. Ashley came to the

house and stayed with him. As you know, Cole has his first theatrical play, which, of course, it being past seven-thirty, we'll miss it, so Ashley went with Cooper to the play." Chad answered. His voice was a lot quieter than usual. I wondered if it was because Kelly was there, if he was worried, or if he was waiting to blow up once we got home.

"Does Cole know anything?" I asked.

"No. Ashley told him we had to work late. I'm sure you'll agree. There's no need to have him flustered and not perform well."

"Of course. That's what I told Ashley to say. He's worked so hard for this part." Tears filled my eyes, "I really wanted to see him perform."

"I'm sure it's been a long day, Shelley. I'm glad you're out. Let's get you home." Kelly said with an empathetic voice.

Chad and Kelly talked a little on the ride home. I barely said a word. I didn't need Chad to call me stupid in front of Kelly and Suzy. Truth be told, I was hoping Cooper wouldn't be affected by being woken up by armed men.

I thanked Kelly again for being there to pick us up and walked into an empty home with Chad still talking to Kelly in the truck. I looked around our beautiful home and wondered if Chad had done anything wrong. Could we lose everything we've built?

Not long after Chad came in, Ashley pulled into the driveway with the boys. Cole came in excited about his performance but wishing he could have done a little better. I smiled as he told the story of his first play. He was so excited. Chad and I had agreed not to tell him anything until the weekend. There was no need to spoil his great night. Ashley went home, and the boys went to bed. After tucking my big boys in, which was just saying good night since they were too big, I went into the bedroom to debrief with Chad.

When I walked in, he had the look of someone without a care in the world. I waited a little while to see if he would check in on me after having spent the entire day being processed like a criminal. I thought maybe he would say he was sorry this happened to me. I thought perhaps he'd hug and hold me so I could let some frustration tears out. He didn't do either of those things.

68

I looked at him in amazement. "You do realize that we got arrested today, don't you? I have never even jay-walked, and I was in jail all day."

"Stop being so dramatic. It's not like you were with a bunch of hardened criminals in a jail cell. The worst thing that happened was you lost out on your creature comforts today."

I couldn't believe it, even though I should have expected it. "Really? I was treated like a criminal, Chad! I didn't do anything to deserve that. Is there something I don't know?"

He walked by me on the way to the master bathroom. "Today sucked. I get it. But don't worry. I'll get it taken care of. We haven't done anything wrong." He turned to keep moving, but then added, "We're in this together, Babe."

He walked into the bathroom and shut the door, leaving me speechless. A strange thought came into my head. *Ever since he started his company, it has been all him. **I** did this, **I** did that, **I** am great, **I** make the money, **I**'m a genius, **I** know what I'm doing, **I** know what's best for you. But now that we went to jail for a day, he's saying **WE** are in this together? Since when did he mention anything business-related as – **we?***

CHAPTER THIRTEEN
"I'LL FIGURE IT OUT!"

The next day began like a typical day – God, how, after just one day, I had missed normal days. I dropped the kids off at school and Chad drove himself to work. A few hours later, I took a call from the Cole's school's Guidance Counselor's office. One of the friends I had called had a daughter Cole's age, and they were best friends. As soon as she saw Cole, she asked him for details about his parents being arrested. That was new news to Cole; he didn't think it was a funny prank. "My parents didn't get arrested. What are you talking about? They're very well respected in the community. Besides, don't you think I'd know if anything like that happened?"

As the minutes and hours passed, he started seeing people staring at him and whispering as he passed them. He was confused. So, he went to the Guidance Counselor to get some clarity on what was going on. I had to tell the Guidance Counselor that it was true and to please tell Cole we were going to tell him about it over the weekend. He went to a small school, and the entire school and staff knew by the time I picked him up. I, too, noticed many stares as I waited in the car line, and even some people took pictures of me on

71

their cellphones. I felt bad for my boys; they shouldn't have had to go through that.

Cole called me the next day in the early afternoon. "Mom, there are people from Child Protective Services (CPS) here. They just interviewed me."

"What?" I couldn't believe it. Shouldn't they get parental permission before interviewing a minor? On top of what, what right did they have to do it at school so others could see?

"They asked all kinds of crazy questions, like, do my parents drink or do drugs, have they been asking strange lately, do they have elaborate parties? Mom, I was even asked if you and Dad had sex in front of me."

Cole was twelve! I was devastated for him. It didn't matter that we didn't do any of the stupid questions they asked him, what mattered was that, without any consent, they could do that. I quickly called Chad to tell him about it. He called me back a little while later. His attorney called CPS and demanded to know the meaning behind them interviewing minors at a school. They told him that because we were both arrested on felony charges, they had the right to interview them without our consent. I was still upset about it.

CPS found no reason to keep an investigation ongoing, so they 'closed our file.' I thought it was overkill with the kids. That organization's mission is to help children; what they did worsened things for mine. Anyone who knows me would know I would never, ever put my kids in harm's way.

Cole was starting to have a hard time focusing on his schoolwork. He started telling me how much he hated the school. When the semester ended, I moved him to a different school at his request. He just couldn't be around it anymore. He was over it. Cooper was less affected. We also gave him the choice of going to another school, but he decided to stay where he was. I don't know if it was because he was a little older or that he had such a tight-knit group of friends, but I was happy he wasn't as affected by it as much.

However, the arrest severely affected Chad's business. News spread that Chad Carter had been arrested on state charges, and none of the title companies he used to do business with wanted to close on any of his properties; the ones he never did business with didn't want too either. That meant, once again, Chad couldn't pay the investors. At first, he thought it was a personal attack, but then he discovered that State officials were telling title companies to back away from him until he cleared his name. Chad was stuck. Some of his projects had just finished, but he had no one to close on them.

"I'll figure this out." He said, as he always did.

Suddenly, he had a brilliant idea. "Look, for some reason, the state wants me in their crosshairs. There's no telling what they're willing to do not to look stupid. I think I will sign everything to the trustee; they will take over all my properties and manage them. In essence, my properties will not be in my name, so the state won't have access to them. And before you say anything, yes, it's one hundred percent legal."

I didn't know enough about Trusts or Trustees, so I just told him to do what he thought was right. He was going to do it anyway. He reached out to a few different attorneys, and they started going over what it would look like if Chad had a Trustee take over the company and the properties. Things got very convoluted. One minute, Chad was telling me he would keep everything away from the state's reach, but a couple of weeks later, he told me that the state said if he also signed over the ranch we owned in Oklahoma, they wouldn't come after us. I didn't know which way was up! *So, is he working against the state or with the state?*

He refused to put the ranch in the deal, but the new attorney advised him that it was his best course of action, so, with much remorse, he threw the ranch in the deal. I asked him if he knew what he was doing. Chad asked his attorney if he could get it in writing but they said no.

"Of course I do. They aren't going to hire someone full-time to manage all this stuff. They asked me, not told me; asked me to please manage the projects because no one knows about them more than I do." He flashed me his best narcissistic smile. "No one can do what I do. You should know that by now."

My heart hurt. He was about to sign all that we – him more

than me – worked for. In a sense, it became a part of our identity. I knew it hurt him more than he let on, but he wouldn't show it. "Do you want me to go with you to the signing tomorrow?" I asked.

"Why? It's all in my name. You don't have to sign for anything."

"I just thought maybe you could use the support. This can't be easy for you."

"It's a strategic move. I can't wait to stick it to them when they see they can't come after what I've earned. I'm okay. Be there for the boys after school."

The next day, Chad confidently signed away our rights to all of our properties, homes, the business, and the ranch he so loved.

The next day, he was locked out of everything he owned.

CHAPTER FOURTEEN
CHAOS AND JESUS

C had received an email early in the morning notifying him that he could not go to the office, the ranch, or any of the properties. The email explicitly let him know that he would be arrested if he even went to any of those places to get family photos. We, well, him more than me, had a lot of personal things at the ranch in Oklahoma: clothes, ATVs, equipment, trucks, and many animals. He even had a customized safe built at the ranch to hold his 80-plus guns. All of it was gone immediately.

He called his attorney in a full-on panic, but he could do nothing. Everything he had built and paid for was no longer his possession. However, what hurt him the most was that he and his "newly former employees" were not allowed to communicate. Most of Chad's waking moments were spent working and with his employees. They were a massive part of his social structure and life. Together, they had done business in the high millions. Now, he was a taboo to them.

With all the new developments going on, I continued asking him if he was sure I didn't need an attorney. He had created some sort of bond with his attorney, but I was out on the cold alone, like in most things in his life. With Chad no longer there to hold order or intimidate, one of his former employees emailed me concerned. The email emphasized that Chad's attorney was not my attorney. The FBI, the SEC, and other law enforcement officers were asking many questions. The person thought of me as a good person and wanted me to protect myself.

Shortly after that, I didn't ask Chad if I should get an attorney; I told him I would get one. Realizing that he couldn't stop it, he did what he did and tried to control it. He had his attorney give us three references. They passed Chad's test and I was allowed to call them. I set up an appointment with a husband and wife team – he handled the cases in court and she dealt with the paperwork and scheduling even though they were both lawyers. I hired the team of Rafael and his wife in January 2019, mainly because I knew I needed to move fast, plus, they seemed like people who would care for me as a person and mother, not just a client.

An atomic bomb hit Chad's business the following month. The Trustee filed Chapter 11 for all of Chad's companies and business dealings. They restructured everything and made them go bankrupt. Chad had no control. One would think that this would break him or silence him, but he stayed the same, claiming he did nothing wrong and that he would beat this bullshit case.

Chad got wind that whoever seized the guns brought them to a local county sheriff's office. Chad had his attorney call the Sheriff's office and was told Chad could get them. He went with his mother, got the guns, and put them in a storage unit in Oklahoma. That was a much-needed win for him; he loved those guns.

As this was going on, my lawyer told me the SEC was making a case to charge him with a civil suit. I told Chad, but he had already known that and told me not to worry about it, while reminding me how much more expensive and better his attorney was. The following month, March of 2019, our bank accounts were frozen. We had lost all access to all our money, even our savings. The SEC went even further and sued him on behalf of the investors who had put up millions of dollars. His attorney told him not to spend money on fighting it. Chad saw it as a witch-hunt and did nothing. The

SEC would later win the civil judgment against him for what he owed the investors.

In that same month of March 2019, there was a search warrant issued on our home. We had a court date scheduled for 9 AM on a Friday. Cole's new school didn't have classes on Fridays, so he was home sleeping when we left. Our court cases were annoying and pointless. They were basically check-ins. They wanted to know we hadn't fled anywhere. We would go in; report, and they would thank us for showing up but that they had to move the date back. However, on this particular date, when we left to go to court, once again, officers armed with tactical gear and AK-47 assault rifles busted the door down and ran into every room in the house with their guns drawn. Cole was woken up to guns pointed at his face!

"Is anyone in the closet?" An officer yelled at him. Cole had just woken up and didn't respond right away.

"What. I don't think so. I was sleeping a second ago."

"Get out of bed. Now!"

"Okay, but can I get dressed?"

They allowed him to dress under supervision, marched him into the living room, and sat him on the couch.

"Is there money behind that art piece on the wall?" He was screamed at / asked.

"Ummm. You can check if you want but I never saw anything."

"Where's the two million dollars? Where do your parents hide it?" Another officer asked.

"We have two million dollars?" Cole answered with a question.

Someone yelled from another room, "I found the safe!"

With all the questions they had asked many people, as I understood it, some people said that we flaunted a bunch of cash and that someone had told them Chad had bragged about having two million dollars in his safe at home. They must have believed it because they wasted a lot of manpower trying to find it.

While this was happening, Chad's attorney got a call that our house was being raided. I called a friend to pick up Cole and to take him to her house and I'll meet them there. Chad and his attorney went to the shit show that was our home. Chad was surprised to see so many people in the house, more than before, including the prosecutor and Agent Rob. They were clearly expecting to find something of monetary value, but all they walked out with were papers, laptops, and computers. When they cleared out, I took Cole home.

I found a busted door and a total mess inside. The door could still shut, but it didn't lock. I couldn't believe our lives had come to this. Not too long before, we were highly respected and valued members of our community; now, we had a busted door, a tarnished reputation, and nothing but closed doors in our faces. (Chad told me he'd fix the front door, but six months went by, and I ended up getting a door company to ensure we could lock the front door).

As for Chad, how did he handle this new stage of our lives? He got himself a new hobby! He went and, without consulting me, of course, bought two Quarter Horses, to compete in cutting horse competitions. They are trained to cut a cow from the herd and prevent it from returning to it. Being that he had experiences with horses, he paid a horse trainer to teach him how to "cut." In actuality, as far as the boys and me were concerned, he stopped leaving every weekend to go to the ranch to start leaving every weekend to go to cutting shows.

As for me, I was still taking the boys to their practices, games, birthday parties, etc. We only went with Chad two times to the cutting horse shows in three years. I saw it all as another excuse for him not to be home on weekends.

He also started taking Cooper to the gym with him during this time after work during the week. They got much closer. It hurt that I saw Cooper pull away from me a little, but I thought maybe it's normal for a boy to grow up closer to his mother, but as he got older, gravitate towards his father. I didn't put much into it. I thought it was a good thing. I loved running and working out, so I was happy Cooper took his health more seriously.

That gave me more ME time and I wasn't sure what to do. I ran at least five miles every morning. My world was in chaos. I had tried all I could, but things continued to spiral downward. I started listening to Christian podcasts, in particular, to Joel Osteen. His positive messages and affirmations helped my head from drowning in negativity. I had to keep it together for the boys. They would see us go to court every month, only to have us tell them our case was delayed again. Each time I went, I wondered if we'd get home to another busted door and searched house.

One morning, while on a run, I slowed to a walk and then a complete stop. I was listening to Joel Osteen again and realized that although I grew up going to church and that as an adult, I'd been active at my church, even attending bible classes; I had never fully given myself to the Lord. I decided then and there to put all my faith in God. "Whatever happens, I will serve you as best I can." Even though things would get worse, it also brought me peace.

In October, we received a certified letter from our personal bank that they were going to close our accounts. We had been with them for more than 15 years! We had taken out various loans and had an impeccable record of paying every cent back on time. I thought they would value clients like us. However, with the SEC freezing our accounts and snooping around, they decided it wasn't worth the hassle. Just like that, we didn't have a checking account. I prayed to God that a bank would allow us to open an account, and thankfully, I was able to find one.

Then, 2020 rolled around, and along with it – COVID-19. The world slowed to a crawl, including the justice system. Not surprisingly, they continued to delay our trial. Chad would have people tell him the police and investigators were asking them questions, looking for more information. They even went to the car dealerships where we got a car to see if we lied in the loan application, saying we made more than we claimed. However, we had paid cash from the sales of our lake and rental properties, so they didn't find anything there either. Chad was convinced that our case continued to get delayed because the state didn't have a case. "Don't worry, they'll drop this charade soon enough. I'll get us through this."

They were looking high and low for incriminating information on Chad, and by default – me! Had I not let Jesus take the wheel, I don't know how I would have gone through those times without a nervous breakdown.

My attorney called to ask questions about Chad. However, Chad

had me just about convinced that my attorney was trying to help me so bad he would do it at the cost of my husband, so I was careful with what I told him. Then, he hit me with what could have been a deal breaker: "The state is saying that your husband has had a girlfriend for quite some time. Are you aware of this?"

I told him Chad and I had a brief separation, but it was years ago, and that I hadn't heard anything like that. Either way, I confronted Chad about it and he denied it. "I told you I didn't trust your attorney!"

"Well, you vetted him for me."

"Ya, but that was before the state got to him. They are stooping mighty low to get us to turn on each other. Me? A girlfriend? If I had one, with all the people I know, someone would have told you about it. Come on, Shelley, think! We'll beat this if we stay loyal and true to each other. They're grasping at straws. This will be over soon."

Just like he always did, he talked himself out of it. However, I called Rafael and asked him if he knew the name of this alleged girlfriend. He told me he didn't. Had he told me a specific name, I would have believed it and left Chad then and there. But, since he didn't, the Carters continued. Chad was flipping houses during the week and going to horse shows on weekends, and I was Cooper and Cole's mom.

And then, something else happened…

CHAPTER FIFTEEN
BEFORE THE TRIAL

2021 rolled around bringing with it more chaos. The boys were very athletic and Cooper had just finished his first year of football. Once he started getting serious working out with his father, Chad talked him into backing off on basketball and do football. He had a decent year for a kid who had never before been too interested in it. However, he was really into working out.

Chad and Cooper decided that Cooper would compete in a body building show. He had five months to train and get his nutrition to the point that he could do well. One of Chad's friends had trained other body builders so he was put in charge of Cooper's training. The thing that dominated my mind during that time was getting all of the calories into my boy. Meal prep was a very present thing. He had to eat 6-7 meals a day.

On the other hand, Cole, who was 14, had been going to boxing classes, started sparring. He would go to group classes and private classes. On one particular private session, his coach had him spar box a young man of 27 years old. As always, I was there. They were given instructions to not go all out, to do more of a contact shadow-boxing, meaning not to throw anything too hard.

They started to spar and I was impressed with Cole. I thought the man would outclass him badly, but Cole looked good in there. Cole landed a nice combination and it upset the man he was sparring. Suddenly, the guy opens up and starts to swing much more aggressively. I had been taking my boys to athletic events all their lives and I'd seen too many parents that overreacted. Cole didn't look my way so I assumed he wanted to continue, so I didn't say anything. When we got home, I showed Chad the footage of the sparring session and Chad got pissed.

He immediately called the coach, "What the hell are you doing putting a fourteen year old against a grown man? Does that guy think he's cool hitting kids? How about I go over there and kick his ass!" That was the last time Cole practiced boxing. He had already started Jiu Jitsu, so we switched him to a gym that was closer. He loved Jiu Jitsu.

Before we knew it, May had come and Cooper had his first body building competition. He had worked so hard and exercised amazing discipline, I just hoped he did well. Well, he did better than well – he won First Place in the Teen Competition!

All he wanted to do when it was over was to eat, the boy looked amazing but he was bone dry on the inside. Chad and I were very proud. Chad started to talk about doing some other competitions. I thought it was soon and that Cooper should take a break before going that hard again. However, his dad wanted him to do more so Cooper went back to serious training and a restricted diet.

Cooper competed in two more bodybuilding competitions, placing 2nd place in one of them. At not winning first, Chad berated his friend who was in charge of training Cooper, telling him that his son was not in the type of shape he should have been. However, Cole told me that Cooper was starving at night and would sneak to the pantry and feast on peanut butter. I was proud of Cooper, who at 17 stayed on such a strict regimen for so long.

TRASH DAY

Life continued on, with the threat of the trial coming up in March of the following year. Towards the end of August, after Chad's birthday, I was gathering the trash on Sunday like I always did because it got picked up Monday mornings. I noticed a box on the driveway and grabbed it to put in the trash. However, when I picked it up, a name jumped out at me – Mercedes Jones!

Could that be the same Mercedes Jones he was dating when we separated eleven years ago? I took a picture of it and threw the box away. I approached him when he got home. From where? I had no clue.

"Hey, so I found a box with Mercedes Jones's name on it. Can you tell me why a box with her name and, what I'm assuming is her new address, on my driveway?

My husband looked straight at me and said, "That's my girlfriend."

I couldn't believe I was hearing those words. There was no remorse, no shame, and no guilt – just a very cocky, straight up jerk attitude.

"What do you mean, girlfriend?"

"That's what I mean. How did you not know?"

"Well for one, when my lawyer told me you had a girlfriend you swore to me up and down that you didn't! How long has this been going on?"

"I don't know, three years, maybe closer to four. I could swear I figured someone would have told you by now."

The matter-of-fact way he told me that he'd been seeing someone behind my back for years was just like he would order a pizza; straight, to the point, no emotion.

"You do know that a person can love more than one person at a time, right?"

Was he trying to get me to accept that he had a girlfriend and I'd remain his loyal wife? "That might be true, but that's not how my life is going to go. Listen to me well, Chad. It would be a bad look for you if I left you now. But as soon as the trial is over, we're getting a divorce. I have stood by your side while you constantly go away, spend money on things I have no idea about, now I'm sure a lot of it was with your girlfriend. And now you think I'm just going to accept it?"

"But Shelley, I love you too."

"We're getting divorced after the trial." I said with as little emotion as I could. I turned and walked away, thinking I had just slipped out of a surreal nightmare. It turned out that everyone in town knew about it. Including his mother. They, the three of them would all hang out. The outright disrespect was too much for me to take.

I got to the bedroom and said, "God, I can't handle this. Please don't let this break me. Give me the strength to go on until the trial."

God didn't answer me, but I am sure He heard me.

Chad tried to be intimate with me several times after. I never slept with him again though. Once he realized I was set to leave him, he decided we should tell the kids. It didn't matter that I wanted to hold off, the tension in the house was insane with the looming trial and the fact that I rarely spoke to him. Yet, he was going to say what he wanted to say.

We called the boys into the living room and Chad told them that we haven't been in a good relationship for quite some time and that we would most likely go our separate ways after the trial. If he expected the boys to cry or plead for us to stay together, he didn't get it. One thing he decided not to mention was that he had a girl-friend for years. I decided not to tell them either. I didn't want to trash their dad to them.

After the conversation, Chad asked me to stay with him until Cole got out of High School. "Divorces are really difficult for kids. You don't want to mess him up, do you?"

"You think I'm going to stay with you for another two and a half years? What you don't get is that if it weren't for the trial, we'd already be getting divorced."

The tension in the Carter home continued to be palpable. Chad would go out and come back late. I wouldn't ask where he was and he wouldn't tell me. He was becoming more involved with the boys and their sports, so they were drifting more to him. I just trusted in the Lord that everything would be all right.

Due to Chad's crazy jealousy, I hadn't had a social media

account for fifteen years. One evening, I decided to create an Instagram account. I got in touch with some old friends and enjoyed seeing their lives through their pictures and posts. Sure enough, a few men slid into my DMs, but I was still married and wasn't interested in a relationship. However, there was one old friend that I communicated with a little more.

Chad threw another fit when he realized I was on Instagram. "You're going to do something to ruin our case!"

"Relax, Chad. I don't think pictures of me with the boys, the dog, and the cat can kill the case."

He asked me repeatedly if I was talking to any guys. I told him that there was one particular guy that I message. "I have the right to know who you're talking to! You're still legally my wife!"

"You've been hiding a girlfriend from me for four years, all the while presenting yourselves as boyfriend and girlfriend all over town when everyone knows we're married, yet you think you have rights to know who I'm talking to?"

He hounded me for days, nonstop. I finally told him who he was. I no longer cared what he thought. Chad knew the guy and, of course, had another fit. "Listen, I'll leave Mercedes. This is crazy. Let's stay together!"

"Chad, after the trial, we're getting divorced. Deal with it."

A few days later he told me that him and Mercedes looked the guy up and did a background check on him. "He's not a good guy. You're in danger. Stop talking to him."

"Wait, you and Mercedes looked him up?"

"Ya. Why?"

"For such a smart guy, you're a total idiot sometimes." I chuckled and walked away.

Another time, he called me and told me his lawyer found out I had an Instagram account and he was right, it could hurt us in the case. I shut it down temporarily, but I reopened it again a week later. Chad wasn't used to me having friends and him not having total control of what I did, who I spoke to, how I spoke, or what I said.

In November of 2021, Cole and I went to Vegas for a Jiu Jitsu tournament. He competed but didn't do that great, however he had only been doing Jiu Jitsu for seven months, about 5/6 days a week. Some people there had been doing it all their lives. We stayed at the MGM Grand. He convinced me to put a hundred dollar bet on a UFC Parlay. I did. The payoff was for $700 the following day.

The next day, I let him sleep in and went to play a little roulette before going to the sports betting area to pick up our winnings. I was up $300 in about twenty minutes. Suddenly, a pit boss came over and asked if I was Shelley Carter.

"Yes, why?"

"I thought you knew. You're banned from here. You need to leave the premises."

"Banned? I haven't been here since 2012 and I didn't cause any trouble then. What do you mean?"

"I was just told to tell you what I told you."

I picked up my chips, cashed them in, picked up our winnings from the sports betting place, and woke up Cole. *Did someone complain I was winning too much? No. $300 is nothing to these people. Wait a minute. Chad had been to Vegas several times without me. The MGM card I was using is issued to him and with me as the secondary user.* I still don't know what Chad did, but I'm sure he got banned from the top casinos in Vegas and never told me about it.

We had an uneventful Thanksgiving and Christmas, with Chad disappearing for hours. I no longer cared what he did. God had given me peace. I just wanted the trial to be over with and to start fresh.

In December, Chad started seeing these life coaches / intuitives. He wanted to know what the outcome of the case was going to be. She told him that he wasn't going to prison. He was seeing one particular woman who, apparently said things he liked. He pressed on me to see her. "First off," I said, "I don't believe in them. Secondly, if I did go, it won't be to the person you see. I'll go to someone that knows nothing about me."

Just like he did with my attorneys, he called around and said he found the perfect guy for me. I made an appointment with him the following week. However, a few days later, he came to the house and told me I didn't have to see him any more.

"Why the sudden change?" I asked.

"I went and saw him today. You know, I had to check him out before you met him. Well, it turns out, the guy is crazy and deranged! I can tell someone's future better than he could. He didn't know anything he was talking about. So, you can cancel those plans."

"No. I made the appointment at your insistence, now, I'm going to see what these people are all about."

I showed up to a guy named Robert's office in Dallas. We began to talk and he let me talk about my mother and grandmother who had passed and how it still grieved me. I was able to share about what was going on and me not having family nearby makes it more difficult. It was good to talk things through.

While I was there, Chad was calling me non-stop and sending me texts. I had my phone on silent in my purse so I didn't realize until after the session. We then talked about Chad and Robert told me I needed to get away from him. "He's been manipulating you and tried to get me to manipulate you into getting off of social media."

I left there in better spirits than when I entered, although I never had a session with Robert again. We did, however talk/text from time to time during the trial. I saw Chad's missed calls and texts and called him back.

"I just wanted to know that you were okay. Why didn't you answer my calls? What kind of crap did he say about me?"

I never told Chad what Robert told me. I had no idea what he would have done to him.

A DEAL

I spent a lot more time with my lawyers as the trial date approached. My attorney's wanted to prep me for taking the stand and wanted to go over any details.

"Shelley, is there anything that's going to come out that we don't know about?"

I thought long and hard. "No. Other than having a text-flirt-emotional-affair that lasted a couple of months, I've told you everything."

Rafael called me one day and asked me to come in. Whatever it was, it was important enough for him to want to tell me in person.

"I don't know who you've been praying to, but you just got a gift. The prosecution is offering to knock the charge down to a misdemeanor. You'll get a $100K fine and would be on probation for only two years. Once the probation is up, it will be deferred from your records. What do you say?"

"Well, in return for what?"

"You'll have to testify against Chad, of course."

"I'll have to think about this."

I called my sister and we spoke at length about the options. If Chad knew I was going to testify against him, he'd kick me out of the house. I also didn't know how the boys would feel if their mother testified against their father. If Chad didn't kick me out, he'd surely turn them against me. At the end, I decided not to take the deal. I knew I hadn't done anything wrong so I wasn't scared of the verdict plus Chad convinced me that he had it all taken care of. I was, however, scared Chad would hurt me some way, most likely through the boys, and I couldn't live without them. Also, even though he drove me crazy at times, Chad was a smart person and I believed him when he said we would be okay.

The trial was set for March 2022. In February, Chad said he was thinking of renting a cabin for a week with the boys after the trial, during Spring Break. He asked me if I wanted to go. I told him most certainly not. I didn't know if his mother or girlfriend was also invited and I didn't care to find out. Either way, I was divorcing him and would be taking the boys to our own trips when the time was right.

My attorney asked me if we had "the talk" with the boys. To get them ready for the worst, if anyone had to do any time.

"No. Chad doesn't think or talk like that. He's expecting to be found Not Guilty and then going on a family vacation!"

CHAPTER SIXTEEN
THE BEGINNING OF
THE END!

"The dog! Where's the dog!"

I came around to see Chad talking to the boys about a picture we have had for seven years.

"Shelley, tell them there used to be a dog in this picture, please."

"Chad, there was never a dog in this picture. What are you talking about?" I asked.

"Are you all crazy right now? How can you not remember the dog?"

He walked away, muttering something about the Mandela effect, how some people can remember things that are no longer the same. I don't know if it was all the drugs I'd find out later he was taking or if it was the stress of the trial. I think, in his mind, an alternate reality had a dog in that picture, and maybe that same alternate reality had a different result from our case. All I thought at the time was that he was starting to lose it.

My attorney prepped me for the trial. I was to wear flat shoes, not heels. I'm already tall; making me taller could look intimidating or imposing, something you don't want to exude when on trial. He told me to wear neutral colors, nothing splashy – "nice pants and a long sleeve sweater" is what he suggested. "Also, no name brands,

89

please." It was a good thing I wasn't into buying name-brand clothes. I did have some big-name purses, but I promised him I'd leave them at home.

We decided to be tried jointly. I wasn't sure it was the best course of action for me, but I had been working with my attorney for almost three years, and he had gained my trust.

Even though the trial dates had been pushed back for years, and we knew of the final trial date for months, the day of the trial seemed to sneak up on me. I felt surreal as soon as I opened my eyes. While preparing myself in the bathroom, thoughts would flash: *How many more times will I be in this bathroom? Are women's prisons as violent as men's prisons? What would the boys do?*

I had walked into courthouses many times. However, this time, the building looked enormous and had an ominous feel. I closed my eyes and prayed for strength. Still, I shuffled into the courtroom like a zombie. My life was on the line. We had made so much money; what good was it now?

The first day was all about selecting the jury. Chad and I sat at a table with our lawyers while the prosecuting attorneys sat beside ours. People filed in with numbers hanging on their chairs. They sat according to a pre-made seating chart with the person's name, age, occupation, and a short bio. Then, the process began. The trial for my freedom had officially started.

A specific judge had been assigned to our case. However, he had another case scheduled for the same time, a murder trial, and he opted to be involved with that one over ours. Our lawyers had requested another date, but the prosecuting attorneys argued that it had been delayed for years and that they were good for the 'sit-in' judge to try our case.

The lawyers asked very specific questions, trying to determine by their answers the people they thought would be more apt to give either a guilty or innocent verdict. Slowly, the 120 potential jurors started dwindling. When it came time for lunch, the attorneys ordered us not to go anywhere a juror might be. He told us not to communicate or even make eye contact with them, or we could get in more trouble. The attorneys ate independently while Chad and I had the prepared peanut butter and honey sandwiches and chips I had brought. We ate lunch near the vending machines, where we got sodas and protein bars.

I expected to have a conversation with Chad about the jurors being let go, but he was too busy making work calls. He was more concentrated on flipping his houses than being involved in the jurors that would decide our fate.

The following day started with opening arguments. I could barely believe what the prosecuting attorney was saying about me. I felt like it was personal for him. He was brutal. He made us look like money-hungry, terrible people that would screw anyone over for money for a buck, even though we were already *rich*.

"The state of Texas will prove, beyond a shadow of a doubt, that Chad Carter was a master schemer and liar and sold securities without a license. We will also prove that Shelley Carter, his wife, who managed all of the money that came into their home and the business, is guilty of laundering money. With the millions of dollars in this case, there is no way that she was not a part of this."

A wave of panic swept over me. *How could someone say things about someone and get away with it in court? Is this really happening?*

Then, something I didn't expect to happen happened. I felt a wave of optimism come over me. I felt a peace that overrode my understanding and fear. God's grace had reached me in the courtroom. I didn't know how, but I knew I would be OK, and the boys too.

CHAPTER SEVENTEEN
THE TRIAL

Chad's attorney gave his opening remarks, and then my attorney gave his for me. I wasn't impressed. He had told me before that he was handicapped in what he could say and do for my defense because Chad and I were being tried together. It wouldn't be a good look if they made him look bad, so there were only so many things he could say.

"I am here to prove that there is no proof whatsoever that Shelley Carter laundered any money. She is not involved in the company's day-to-day proceedings. While she managed the books, the biggest investment of her time and energy was spent on being a great mother to two very active boys. I will show you the paper trail of emails that directed her on what to do with the finances..."

Again, I wasn't impressed.

The state called their first witness, a financial analyst. She talked about their investigation to see where the money had come from, how we had gotten it, and where it went. Our attorneys caught her a few times not really knowing her numbers or having all the facts straight. They went back and forth. During this time, Chad would tap his attorney on the shoulder, making him turn around and adamantly tell him questions to "get her."

After several taps, his attorney got agitated and told him, "Write it down and pass me a note. You have to stop continually tapping us on the shoulder. You seem panicked to the jury."

However, Chad continued to get their attention. He was so controlling that he had to get his two cents in. He felt he knew more than his lawyers anyway. While at home, during the trial, he would tell me things like, "It's not that they're dumb, but this is my life, and who knows better how to defend my life than me!" When I would suggest that he follow their lead, he would say, "They work for me, not the other way around. I tell them what to do, they don't tell me."

When the woman got off the stand, I felt they had done a good job discrediting her. My optimism increased slightly. Then, several investors came up, one after the other. They each told the court how much money they lost and how Chad had guaranteed them a ten percent interest. The lawyers brought home that there are no guarantees in any real estate, so even to suggest it is, at the very least, manipulating, if not outright lying.

They proved he had provided them with false information. He lied to them in the brochure, which stated he had a Chemical Engineering Degree from Virginia – which was untrue. He had told them he toured with Robert Kiyosaki, from Rich Dad Poor Dad fame, which was false. He also told them he worked for Texas Instruments, which was untrue. They testified that Chad showed them plans and took some of them to the land where he was going to build, which he was not legally able to do.

The day started to wear on, and the questions started getting repetitive to those testifying against us:

"Did he tell you it was backed by real estate?"

"Yes."

"That was a lie. Did he tell you there was no risk involved?"

"Yes."

That was a lie. "Did he tell you he was a Chemical Engineer?"

"Yes."

"That was another lie. Did he tell you he toured with Robert Kiyosaki?"

"Yes."

"That was another lie. Did he tell you that he once worked for Texas Instruments?"

"Yes."

"That was another lie. Did he tell you…"

Every person said yes to the questions. I was observing the jurors more than the people on the stand. They were making Chad out to be an evil mastermind who swindled people out of millions. In a way, I wished the boys were there so they could see how the trial was going for themselves. I started to get kind eyes from jurors and watched their expressions change when they looked at him. I was hoping they could figure out who the mastermind in this was.

Then, they started asking them what he said about me.

"Did he tell you Shelley Carter had a degree in accounting?"

"Yes." "Yes." "Yes." "Yes." "Yes." "Yes."

They all said yes. I wanted to scream at him. I had never told anyone I had a degree in accounting! I heard him say that one time and told him not ever to say it because it wasn't true. He had retorted that numbers were the one thing I was really good at, and since I had done it for years, I was better than people with a degree in accounting, so why not just say it? He had a way of rationalizing anything he said or did.

Every investor talked about the money they gave and how much they got back. One was an elderly gentleman who invested so that he could have enough money for medical problems he needed to take care of. They all averaged getting back about eighteen cents for every dollar they gave him. One investor put in more than a million dollars and got back two hundred thousand.

It did not look good for him, and because we were being tried together, for me either. Then, Tom was brought in to testify, the one who started Chad down the wrong path. He was guided in wearing shackles on his feet, handcuffs, and a green jumpsuit. He had been in jail since 2018, only four years ago, but had aged terribly. I started to think that it was over for Chad.

But when they asked Tom if he could identify Chad, the defendant, he was unable to do so, even though anyone could guess who

95

Chad was just by where he was sitting. Our lawyer got Tom to admit he had dementia. "Is that why you're just agreeing with everything the prosecutors ask you?"

"I guess so."

Our attorneys made a good case that with two people's futures lying in the balance because he was suffering from dementia, Tom's testimony could not be taken under serious consideration.

I felt the day hadn't gone great, but it ended well for us. I hoped Tom's incoherent testimony would be the last thing on the jury's mind as we walked out.

We went home that evening, and he would get right into work mode, talking to different people on the phone.

"Dad, how'd it go in court?" Cooper asked him when he got off the phone.

Chad smiled. "It's going great. The prosecutors don't have a case. They are looking dumber and dumber. They don't have what it takes to outsmart me. So, keep your head in school and don't worry about me. They're clutching at straws. Us Carter boys don't lose." The boys smiled and he returned to his phone calls.

I wanted to tell the boys that ninety percent of trials were found guilty, and I thought our chances, more that Chad's chances, looked slim after it was proven in court that he was a chronic liar. But he would have found a reason to scold me and continue to try to distance the boys from me.

The trial continued with more witnesses called up by the prosecutors, including Agent Rob. When our attorneys cross-examined him, they asked why he went to our home with guns, knowing one of our teenage boys was home.

"We were informed that he had many guns and was considered dangerous," Rob answered. I kept a straight face for the jury but felt like that was another small win for the prosecution.

CHAPTER EIGHTEEN
THE VERDICT

The judge made it clear that he wanted the trial wrapped up by Friday. During the week, my attorneys made it a point to separate me from Chad when conferring with me, as if to clarify that even though we were tried together, I was my own person and had a separate case.

During a break, my attorney told me, "Shelley, we are negotiating separately with the prosecutors. If somehow the jury thinks you were intricately involved in all of this and they find you guilty, I'm pretty sure we can negotiate probation for you."

I closed my eyes and thanked God.

"I wouldn't mention this to Chad, of course." He said. I never mentioned it to Chad.

The prosecutors brought in tons of paperwork – emails, contracts, etc. for the jury to examine. They also went to mid-Thursday in presenting their case, giving us one afternoon to fight for our freedom. The reality was, however, that we didn't have many people testifying on our behalf.

The first person to testify for us was our CPA. She said she never saw any red flags and never had issues with the accounting. We paid our taxes correctly every year and were a pleasure to work with. She made me look good in front of the jurors. I wanted to mouth her a 'thank you' as she walked by and smiled and nodded to me as she walked by me.

Then they called our old lender, the guy Chad used before he started working with Tom. The lender said Chad and he worked on over twelve hundred loans.

"How many loans did Chad not pay back?" His lawyer asked.

"Chad paid off every loan. I never had an issue with him making payments in all twelve hundred loans."

The prosecuting attorney asked him, "If you had such a great working relationship with Chad, why did he start using another lender?"

He answered, "I won't speak for him, but I think it was because he wanted more loans, and I didn't have the bandwidth to keep up with his demands."

"So, he stopped working for you because he got greedy?"

Chad's lawyer stood up. "Objection, your honor."

The prosecuting attorney smiled and said, "Withdrawn. No further questions."

There it was, said aloud for everyone to hear. Chad got greedy. Of course, the judge told the jury not to pay attention to that, but how does someone unhear something they heard?

As the trial came to a close, my attorney told me Chad was adamant about testifying for himself. We weren't in the room with him and his attorney, but the way he told me made it look like they got into quite a spirited conversation/argument. "My life is on the line here, and you're not letting me fight for myself? Whose side are you on? Why do I pay you?"

I would guess there were plenty of F-Bombs in that conversation, but again, I wasn't there. I was surprised his attorney won that argument and Chad didn't testify. I know it bothered him a great deal not to show everyone how smart he was.

The trial went by fast. It wasn't a dramatic event. There were no huge revelations or many ooh's or aaah's. The prosecutors focused most of their time on getting Chad. At one point, they tried to get me to testify against him and offered me a deal, but I refused. I never told Chad about that either. Even in his closing argument, the only thing the prosecutor said about me was that because I was Chad's wife, I must have known what he was doing, so I was complicit. He went on and on about Chad but only said one or two sentences against me.

We wrapped up the trial at 3 PM Thursday. Our attorneys returned from talking to the judge and told us that he ordered the jurors to stay and deliberate until they came up with a verdict. They had stacks of paperwork to go through, so we thought we would wait at the courthouse for a while. We went to sit in one of the side rooms as the jurors decided our fate.

"I'm going to the truck to get some fresh air. Want to come?" Chad asked me. I wondered if this was the last time I'd ever be alone with him. I realized again that I didn't want anything to do with him. He had lied to me for years, had done nothing but put me down, tortured me emotionally for the last ten years, had a girlfriend for years without telling me, and he even lied to our boys about me. I had no desire to share the same fresh air with him.

"No, thank you," I said and turned from him. He went out, and I wondered if he would run and not come back. He must have known that the trial did not go well for him. However, he came back with a smile, waiting to be declared innocent and take the boys and his girlfriend on a vacation.

We were summoned back to the courtroom at 5 PM. During the trial, there was one bailiff in the courtroom, but when we got there, there were five, each wearing guns and a protection vest. I wondered what was going on in Chad's mind when he saw them.

Then, the jury came in and I forgot about Chad and thought about my fate. My attorney told me again, "Remember, no matter what they say, don't react." I nodded and closed my eyes. *Am I really going to lose my freedom and not raise my boys? Lord, please don't fail me now.*

Peace came over me again, and I braced for whatever God had in store for me. It was like having an out-of-body experience, almost like watching the filming of a movie instead of this being my real life.

A bailiff barked, "All Rise!" The judge came in, and my mind raced. I was standing there with the man I had loved for so long. *How did everything go so wrong?*

The head juror stood up with a paper in her hand. The judge asked, "In the case of the state of Texas against Chad Carter on selling securities illegally, what did the jury decide?"

"On the count of illegally selling securities, we fine find Chad Carter – Guilty."

I didn't react, and neither did Chad.

"On the case of the state of Texas against Shelley Carter on counts of money laundering, how did the jury decide?"

Everything was moving too fast! The head juror glanced at me and then read from her paper:

"On the count of money laundering, we find Shelley Carter – Guilty."

CHAPTER NINETEEN
BOND HEARING

I didn't move. I couldn't if I wanted to. My mind was clinging to the hope that the prosecutor would still recommend probation for me even after I chose not to testify against Chad. Then, things happened even faster.

The judge dismissed the jury and ordered the bailiffs to take Mr. Carter into custody. They reached for him, but he raised his hands so they couldn't hold them. "Can I give my wife the things in my pocket and my rolling bag?" He asked, annoyed. "It's not like I can run anywhere."

The judge told the bailiffs to hurry up and get him in custody. Chad emptied his pockets and put a wad of cash on the table, along with his wallet, phone, watch, and keys. As the bailiffs put his arms down and put him in handcuffs, he kicked over his rolling bag to me.

They took him to a side door, and I heard him very nicely say to a bailiff that the cuffs were too tight. Then, he was out of sight.

I looked at the stack of money he left. It was three thousand dollars. He always had to be a hot shot, the big dog, the king of the hill. I wondered how that would work out for him in prison.

Still on his chair, the judge asked the attorneys, "What about Mrs. Carter, gentlemen?"

The prosecuting attorney said, "We are negotiating something for her and ask that she be allowed to go home until we can present it."

The judge looked at me. "You are free to go. Have a good night, Mrs. Carter."

I thanked him aloud and thanked God in my head. My attorneys surrounded me and walked me out of the courtroom and into a side room.

"I can't believe they found you guilty, Shelley, but don't worry. The prosecutor wants Chad's head, not yours. They have agreed to request probation for you, so you won't see the inside of a prison as long as you don't get into trouble. However, in return, they want you to testify tomorrow morning at Chad's bond hearing."

"You want me to testify against my son's father?"

"It's either that or he takes you down with him; I wish there were another way."

I got in my car, which was parked next to Chad's truck, and drove home, leaving the truck and wondering what I would tell the kids. I called them and told them to meet me at home. They were both outside the house, waiting for me.

Cole looked at the driveway, as if expecting to see the truck. "Where's dad?"

I got them in the house and told them everything, "Boys, Chad and I both were found guilty."

Cooper is a lot like me because he doesn't have big reactions and instead internalizes things first. Cole is more like his father and is more boisterous about his feelings. I told them that they had taken their dad into custody and were probably going to give me probation. "However, in return, they want me to testify against Chad."

Cole got very upset and started crying. "Mom, you can't do that to dad! You can't go against the family like that."

"Would you rather I go to jail? I didn't do anything. Your father got me in this mess. You have to be fair to me, too!"

Cooper looked numb, like he couldn't believe what he was hearing. Just the day before, his father was bragging about beating this trumped-up charge and taking them on a fun-filled vacation, and now his mother was going to testify against his father so he wouldn't get bonded out until the sentencing. They thought their father was being treated unjustly. They thought I was treating him unjustly.

"They consider him a flight risk and a threat to me and those who testified against him. Your dad has told you himself about the guys he's beaten up, about how he told people off and put them in their place. I didn't do that to him, he did it to himself."

We went back and forth, but in the end, just like I didn't win in court, I didn't win at home. The boys were upset with me, as if I had done this to the family. Chad had two phones because he thought people were tapping into his conversations. Cole came into the bedroom and asked for his dad's phones. I found it an odd request but handed him the phones.

I woke up the next morning surprised to see the boys already awake. I told them that they were free to come to the courtroom if they wanted to. Cole had Fridays off from school, but not Cooper. They both chose to go. As I was still getting ready, I heard the door open. I went towards the front door and saw them getting into Chad's' mother's car, carrying his two phones and other items she must have asked them take from me. There was no doubt that she made me look like the bad guy in this situation, and there was nothing I could do about it.

When I got to the courthouse and went to park next to Chad's truck, I saw that every door was open. Chad had a safe in his truck, and the boys and their grandmother were ransacking it but all the items from the truck were gone. The girlfriend had come the night before and pulled everything out of the truck using the keypad to get in. I parked next to the car, got out, and asked what they were looking for. None of them answered me. They closed the truck and went with their grandmother.

It hurt my heart deeply. Even though I was determined to divorce Chad, I had been through a very emotional and draining ordeal, and there was a chance the judge wouldn't accept the prosecutor's deal and send me to prison. I had no one to hug, no one to tell me everything was going to be okay outside of my sister, who was in another country.

"You have to do what you have to do to survive and be there for your kids," she told me over the phone. "They're young and are at the point of losing their father; keep loving them; they'll come around. I promise. It's time for someone to finally fight for you, and that someone is you."

I held my head high and walked into the courtroom. I was surprised to find my lawyer waiting for me at the top of the escalators. He brought me to a side room. "We're talking to the prosecutors, and they're still willing to offer that deal to the judge. But I want you to know, Cooper, Cole, and your mother-in-law are already in the courtroom. Judging by their faces, they're not happy."

My attorneys left to talk to the prosecuting attorneys and came back into the side room. They told the judge you are here and willing to testify against your husband not to be let out on bond because he has been violent and vindictive in the past, has access to firearms, and a pattern of violence. They also believed he was a flight risk. The judge said he would not make you testify against your husband in front of your kids. He has ruled that Chad is denied bail until the date of his sentencing."

I was so relieved. I did not doubt that Chad would have come for me some way, somehow. But more than that, I had been a nervous wreck about testifying against my son's father in front of them. Once again, God had intervened.

I left the room and looked into the courtroom, but the boys were gone. I went outside and found that Chad's truck was also gone.

I let out a long sigh. *What is my future ex-mother-in-law up to now?*

CHAPTER TWENTY
CIVIL WAR

I got home and saw Chad's truck in the driveway, and my kids coming in and out of the house packing some of his belongings into their grandmother's car. I went in, and they walked past me, bringing their father's jewelry and other items their grandmother specifically asked for, such as the thirty or so pairs of exotic boots Chad had. I didn't care. I didn't want them.

Then I heard my mother-in-law tell Cooper to get in the truck. I got in my car and blocked him from leaving the driveway. "You can't leave with the truck," I tried to explain, "The attorneys said not to move any assets until we talk to them. I can't move or even sell it if I wanted to."

"I'm not going to give you the chance to sell it. Cooper is going to drive it to Oklahoma for me!" She said.

"I have no intention of selling it. I'm just letting you know that you might get charged if you take this vehicle. The prosecutor's said not to move any assets." I warned.

"This is his truck, not yours!" She yelled.

"The trust owns the truck, not him," I answered calmly.

"I can't believe you were going to testify against him. After the life he gave you? Look at your house? Look at your car? After he broke his back providing you with anything you could ever want, you were going to testify against him? How dare you?"

I smiled. At least I knew the nonsense she was feeding my kids. "Anything I could ever want? He's always done everything he wanted. He was emotionally and mentally abusive to me for years. He…"

"You're making that up!" She interrupted.

"Did I make up that he had a girlfriend for years behind my back? Did I want that too? Did I want that you, my mother-in-law, knew he had a girlfriend for years and, not only did you not tell me about you condoned it. You knew about it all along and never told me." She didn't answer and looked away, nervously. I walked up to her calmly, my confident steps were the only things that were audible.

"I am going to let everyone know what transpired in our relationship. You weren't there day in and day out in my house. The court just exposed the type of son you raised. But wait, maybe you have no clue who your son really is."

The kids ended up leaving in her car with overnight bags. I called them several times but they didn't answer. Finally, Cole texted me back and told me they were staying at a hotel with their grandmother.

I was lost in a big house by myself. My husband had been found guilty, he was in prison, and his mother, who preferred his girlfriend on the side over his legal wife, was poisoning my boys. I fell asleep on pillows wet from tears.

～

Cole had a Jiu-Jitsu tournament the following day. I offered to pick him up. He agreed but made it clear that he was angry with me and didn't want to talk about his dad, his dad's girlfriend, his grandmother, or anything about the trial. We rode mostly in silence, but I just was glad to be with him.

We got to the tournament and my mother-in-law approached

me with a grin. "Hey Shelley, Mercedes is here. Do you want to meet her?"

By then, I had known that Chad had told Cooper about Mercedes six months before the trial. He had also told Cole about her a month before the trial, and they had gone bowling together. Now, she was at his tournament, and my mother-in-law was smug about it.

"No, I'm good."

"You do know that she's always going to be in Chad's life, right? They love each other. Because Chad finally found true love, she's going to be in your boys' lives forever."

"We'll see how long that lasts," I said and walked away. Thankfully, I didn't see her at the tournament.

The kids returned home that day but were clearly still mad at me. Occasionally, one would say, "Why would you do that to Dad? Meme is right; you were the one who's been lying to us."

I had defended myself over and over again to them but each time, it fell on deaf ears. Somehow, their innocent, loving, always-there-for-them-dad was in prison and it was their lying-mom's fault. I contacted a friend named Eric, who had done some house flips with Chad. He had called me after the trial to check in on me and told me that he had talked to five different people about stories of the same incident Chad had told them and got five different versions. I asked if he would mind coming over to talk to the boys.

He came over, prepared with stacks of papers for the boys to see. He shared with them the things he had personally seen Chad do and the things people told him he had done. He had physical proof to defend some of the stories. The boys had no way of disputing what they heard and saw. Slowly it started dawning on them that perhaps their dad wasn't telling them the entire truth.

Still, the boys and I had some pretty emotional conversations.

"But mom, he would tell us in front of you that you had cheated on him, and all these crazy stories, and you never defended yourself?"

"No matter what I'd say, he would find a way to flip it. You guys were too young to remember the crazy arguments your dad and I had when I would stick up for myself. Once you guys got older, it wasn't worth it."

I told them I figured they'd figured out who the liar was. "To know a person, you must see their actions and patterns. Your father says he works all of the time, which is why he's not home. Yet, when he finally has free time on weekends, he's not here! He's gone every weekend! Is that true or not?" They didn't answer but they didn't have to. We all knew I was telling the truth.

I continued, "Look at my patterns. I put your interests ahead of mine. If you have someplace to go, I change any plans I might have to take you there. Where am I on weeknights? Where am I on weekends? Where am I every morning? When would I have the time to entertain all the men he says I have? When you call, I answer. When you text me, I text you right back. I'm either at home or with one of you!"

"Why wouldn't you say that in front of him, though...." They were having a tough time understanding that their dad wasn't the hero he made himself out to be. They didn't want to, and I didn't blame them for that.

"I didn't feel the need to defend myself against your father's crazy stories. Not to the people who know me better than anyone. I raised you boys. You know me."

We came to a cold stalemate that lasted several weeks. We weren't talking much, but their dad, grandmother, and Mercedes called them every day. I repeatedly quarreled with my sons about telling them how much it hurt me and that I wished that at least they wouldn't talk to Mercedes, but I decided to let them handle their relationships themselves. While those three continued to feed them lies, I had to lean on the fact that I had raised good kids and let God fight for me.

One day, Cooper told me, "Mom. I thought I'd let you know. We told Mercedes to stop calling us."

"Really?"

"Ya, she started saying things dad had said, that you had been running around on him and that he was lonely, and she saw what a great person he was, even though you couldn't see it anymore. We just got tired of hearing the same lies."

"Both of you asked her to stop?"

"Ya, but she wouldn't. So we blocked her. Then she tried to contact us through her daughter's phone."

"And what did you guys do?"

"We blocked that phone number too!"

I felt God smiled at me and told me; *Thanks for letting Me work that out for you.*

CHAPTER TWENTY-ONE
THE AFTERMATH

One would think there would be a lull between the trial and the sentencing, but that couldn't be further from the truth. My attorneys instructed me to file for divorce after the trial immediately. They did not have to convince me. He had paraded his girlfriend around his mother, his sister, his employees, all around town, and in front of my two boys. I took some divorce attorney referrals and immediately began making calls and setting appointments. I hired an attorney and started the divorce proceedings less than two weeks after the trial.

Many years prior, Chad made me get off social media, telling me that it was a waste of my time. I realized that it was one of his tactics to isolate me from everyone. I got on Instagram in the fall of 2021 and quickly caught up with some of my high school friends. My sister and I are only 14 months apart and have many mutual friends. One of them was Stephanie, my former best friend, who Chad had lied about nearly twenty years before. I mentioned to some mutual friends that I wanted to reach out to her but I didn't know how she would feel about it. One of our friends talked to her and she told him it was okay to give me her number.

I was nervous about calling her, but I really felt the need to apologize for believing him over her back then. Now that he had proven to be an even bigger liar than I thought, I knew he had lied about her. I found the courage to call her in April, and we had a long, in-depth, honest conversation.

"Please forgive me for not believing you," I pleaded. "I had no idea who he really was at the time, and I'm sorry to have caused you any pain."

"That was a long time ago; we were much younger then. It did hurt because you were my best friend in the whole world. However, I trusted that you would eventually know the truth in God's timing." Her father had been a pastor for more than 40 years, and she strongly believed in God. We picked up where we left off, and the special bond I thought was broken quickly repaired itself – as if we were back on God's time.

We finally got to see each other in person in May of 2022. I went to her house and we had a great lunch. It felt great to be with her again. After, she called her stepbrother, Richard, to take a look at a leak in her bathroom. I had also known Richard since high school. Stephanie's mother had married Richard's father, so they were family now. It was great to see Richard again, and his smile. The three of us went to dinner and reminisced about high school and told each other what we had known about mutual friends.

I felt so alive, so much like an adult, talking to real friends, not just people that Chad told me I could. Richard and I exchanged numbers and he texted me the next day. We began texting and calling daily. He was a pillar of strength for me during such an exhausting time. Then, one day, he asked me out. I hadn't thought of nothing but raising my kids and keeping Chad content enough to not yell at me for years, romance was definitely not something I had considered. However, Richard was great company... and he did have a great smile. I said yes and we've been dating ever since.

I also reached back out to Eric, who had graciously taken time out of his life to talk to my boys about Chad. I had done some accounting work for him part-time, basically whenever Chad asked me to. I told Eric I needed a job as soon as possible. If he had a full-time position that would be awesome.

"Well, it's actually a good time for me. I can certainly use an assistant. You can do the accounting, which I already know you're great at, and also meet with clients and help them with their plans for the house we're building for them."

"I don't need a pity job, Eric…"

"It's not for pity! You have already worked on my books, and if you can do other assistant work, you'll be helping me out."

Chad hit the roof when he found out I was working for Eric. One of the boys told him when he called them from county Jail. He threw a tirade, telling him that Eric was HIS contact and who does Eric think he is and Eric is trying to fill my shoes at work and now he's making a move on my wife, and a bunch of other nonsense. He also reached out to Eric personally, probably to threaten him about me working for him, but Eric never took his call.

I was in the car one time when Chad called Cole. "It's Dad," he said, as if asking if it was okay for him to take the call.

"Answer if you'd like. He's your father," I said.

I couldn't hear what was said, but I soon heard Chad's voice – he was shouting at Cole about something.

"I don't know. I'm not asking her anything, Dad. I don't want to be in the middle of it."

Chad barked something at Cole, and Cole answered, "I answered because you're my dad!"

Cole took the phone from his ear, and we both heard Chad yell, "Well, you need to let me know right now!"

Cole brought the phone to his face and said, "I don't want to get involved." His father hung up on him. The more the boys talked to him, the more they realized that he was a chronic liar and how bad of a temper he had. The boys had seen his temper, but whenever he was with them, he was always the fun dad, the rich dad, and the hero dad. This was a different person than the one they idolized. The more they realized the truth about him, the less they wanted to speak with him. Sadly, for their relationship, the calls started to become less and less frequent.

However, it was not sunshine and rainbows for us. A new war at home began. Cooper had always been a great student. However, the fiasco of his parents' trial, people discussing it on the news, and articles written in newspapers and online magazines, became too much for him, and it affected his schoolwork.

I had to bicker with him to get up and go to school. He'd talk back, telling me I didn't understand what he was going through. Then I started to get concerned teachers calling me, telling me that he'd never had a problem turning in work, but lately, he hadn't turned anything in, and they were concerned.

One of his coaches even called me to see how he could help. "Cooper's been such a good, responsible kid since I've known him. If you'd like, I will coordinate with his teachers and make sure he's turning in his work and taking the tests needed to graduate." I was grateful for their support, but we couldn't get through to Cooper, no matter what we tried. His grades were plummeting, and many of us were worried.

One day, someone from the school's administrative office called to tell me Cooper didn't show up to school. I had (still have) the Life 360 app, which I used on my boys, and it showed me his location. "Are you sure someone didn't make a mistake and said he's absent? I'm looking at his location and he's at the school."

"I don't think anyone's made a mistake, Mrs. Carter; more than one teacher marked him absent."

I drove to the school and saw him sitting in his truck. He was having a very hard time processing the family's changes. It was a dark time for all of us, especially him.

At the same time, my mother-in-law would call the boys and ask them to do something for her or get something and sneak it to her. After the first day, when they brought her a bunch of Chad's things and basically blew me off, they didn't feel good being asked to do anything like that again. Their Meme replied with, "If you don't do anything for me, I won't do anything for you!" The boys were starting to get sick of that, too.

At the end, Cooper is a strong young man and was able to pull it together and graduate. It was right before the summer, so my sister from Dubai was in town; my new-old best friend Stephanie was also there to see my oldest son graduate high school. It was a total victory for our little family.

However, life was still challenging. Chad had given his mother Power of Attorney over his assets, whatever they were. She was probably the only one who knew of any money Chad may have hidden away. I had started working for Eric but I was still in a bind. Chad had only put enough money in every month to pay the bills. All of the business accounts were gone. He would buy gold, silver, watches, and guns that his mother had in her possession.

I can never be sure, but I would not have put it past him to buy many assets and put them in his mother's and girlfriend's names. All I know is that I didn't have it, and as soon as he knew I was going to testify against him after the trial for the sentence hearing, he left me on financial life support. The mortgage alone was six thousand dollars a month, and my new boss certainly wasn't paying me that much.

If I wanted to get my vengeance, I had my chance – the hearing was right around the corner, and I was definitely going to testify.

CHAPTER TWENTY-TWO
CHAD'S SENTENCING HEARING

I woke up a nervous wreck. I knew what I had to do and that I was doing the right thing, but when someone gets married, and if they're like me, they take the vows seriously. For richer or poorer, in sickness and in health, and till death to us part. Not only was I actively divorcing my husband, in several hours I would testify against him in court.

Thankfully, I had plenty of support. My sister came with me, as did Stephanie. As great as that was, and as much as I will always appreciate their support, the biggest boost I got was from my sons. We had gone through so much the last few months. For a while, they wouldn't speak to me, believing I had done horrible things behind their father's back. However, as time had gone on, and through several open conversations, they realized the person I was, was totally different than the person their father, his mother, and his girl-friend were telling them I was. They, too, came to support me. Because of all of them, I felt invincible.

The courtroom was an undeniable account of how people felt about Chad. The prosecution side: my side, had a bunch of people. The defendant's side; Chad's side had some of his family. I assumed my mother-in-law, his aunt and Chad's girlfriend would testify, so they couldn't be allowed in until that time.

My attorney met me in a side office prior to the Sentencing Trial. "Shelley, I don't know Chad, but I know him enough to know he's going to try to intimidate you by staring you down. Keep your focus. In fact, keep your eyes on me. Everything's going to be ok, just say the truth. Can you do that?"

"Yes," I smiled. God was also supporting me and I wasn't scared. "I can."

They called several people before me, but finally, my name was called. I walked into a hushed courtroom. As I walked by where Chad sat, he snickered something to his lawyer. I didn't know if I felt like running out or smiling. I did neither. I just sat down and got sworn in.

"Shelley, can you point out your husband for the court?"

I looked right at Chad, raised my right arm, and pointed my finger at him. I wanted to say, "Soon to be ex-husband," but instead I just pointed at him with an unwavering, steady hand. I think he must've known right then that he was in trouble.

The prosecuting attorney started asking me basic questions like when did we get married, what we did for work, and then his questions got more detailed into Chad's work and my role as the bookkeeper.

"Is it true that your current house was purchased for $1,250.000?"

"Yes."

"How much was the ranch worth?"

"Three million dollars."

They displayed a picture of our house, with the pool, our cars, and the ranch. It truly was a sprawling estate. Instead of being proud to live there, I felt embarrassed that we lived in such a house while Chad owed people millions of dollars.

"Is it true Chad recently bought a brand-new truck?"

"Yes."

"What type of truck?"

"A Ford F-250."

"Is it true that he is an active horse cutter?"

"Yes."

"Can you tell the court the average amount of money he spends a month on his horse hobby?"

"Anywhere from fifteen thousand to twenty thousand any given month."

"How do you know?"

"The last check I wrote for the horse facility was for fifteen thousand dollars."

"It's been proven in this court that Chad has many, many guns. What would you estimate his gun collection to be worth?"

"It would be a guess on my part. However, I know the cost of some of them, so I would estimate his gun collection is worth at least seventy thousand dollars."

"Let's switch topics and talk about his alleged temper and violent tendencies…"

As the questions kept coming, I noticed a face staring at me maliciously through the window to the hall. It was Chad's girlfriend, hating me. I motioned to my lawyer and he came to get me water. When he got near, I told him a woman was staring me down from the hallway. He quickly approached a bailiff and asked him to tell the woman to stop trying to intimidate me and to get away from the door. Soon after, Chad's girlfriend moved from the door. That was the last time I ever saw her.

Chad tried as hard as he could to participate in my questioning. Sometimes he'd throw his hands up and blow wind loudly to let everyone know he was exasperated. Sometimes he would chuckle and shake his head, as if to show I was lying. Other times, he would squint his eyes and glare at me. After he would do any of those things, I would look at my boys and they would nod at me, as if to let me know it was okay, I was doing a good job, and to keep going.

They questioned me for thirty-five minutes. I answered every question truthfully. Chad had stolen a lot of money from a lot of people. People might have thought that I did reap from his actions, but truth be told, he wanted the house, he wanted me to drive the car he bought me, and he was in control of all the money. I would wake up, see the boys through their days, eat dinners with them or at home, run, and sleep. I didn't have a luxurious line of the most expensive handbags, I didn't have 150 pairs of shoes, I didn't treat people to the finest restaurants or rack up hundreds of dollars in bar tabs, nor did I have a wardrobe worth more than Chad's watch collection. He had married a simple, honest, scared to do anything wrong girl and that's exactly who I still was.

I was allowed to stay in the courtroom after I was done. I walked by him for the final time, looking at my boys smiling at me. I went and sat in between them as the hearing continued. I was the last one who testified for the prosecution, so as soon as I sat down, Chad's attorney called his first of two witnesses – his mother.

She was asked where he would live if he was let out. She answered he could live with her. She was asked what type of relationship she had with me, her daughter-in-law, and she answered that we had a great relationship until I filed for divorce. I held in a laugh. I hoped the prosecuting attorney would follow up by asking her if that's she also got along well with Chad's girlfriend or something, but, of course, he never did.

She took the liberty to tell the court that Chad can only pay people back if he was working, not in jail. She also explained that he was a great person, a great family man – which I don't think worked out well being that his wife and kids were sitting on the opposing side. Finally, she talked about Chad's military service and how her father was a 20-year military man who then went to work on the police force.

I was half-expecting someone else to be called, since I hadn't come into the courtroom until I got called. However, the only other person to be called to testified on his behalf was his aunt, his mom's sister. Chad found himself in a situation he said he would never face; his fate was in the hands of a Texas judge.

After a brief recess, we were all ushered in the courtroom to hear the sentencing. We all entered as the judge walked into the room and we all sat down right after he sat down. This was the single most important moment in Chad's life, and as my husband for many years, mine too, and as the father of my kids, theirs too.

The judge opened up by saying he found it disturbing that after being arrested on 6 charges and out on bail, and then having three and a half years to start to make things right with those he owed, Chad didn't make a single attempt to do the right thing.

"You've had ample opportunity, Mr. Carter, instead you continued to live a life of excess, which I find incredibly disrespectful to your investors. I hereby sentence you to pay twenty-nine million dollars in restitution, and I sentence you to forty-five years in prison."

The boys and I froze in shock.

CHAPTER TWENTY-THREE
MY SENTENCE HEARING

I went to bed wondering how I would feel the following month as I prepared to go to my sentencing hearing. I was grateful to God that I didn't have any nerves or anxiety. It was a typical morning, with me preparing the boys and myself. I assured them I was fine and they didn't have to come with me. I had support in that my sister and Stephanie had already told me there was no way they wouldn't be there.

"Besides, the judge said he would take whatever the lawyers agree to, and they've agreed to no prison time, so it's already a win."

Prior to the sentencing, the court had me take a psychological evaluation assessment test. It was more to show proof I wasn't making up the emotional and mental abuse I suffered at the hands of Chad. They gave me a list of places to visit, and I paid $1,200 for the evaluation.

During the counseling session, they showed me a visual of The Domestic Violence Wheel. I was able to see that Chad, in one form or another, had done everything to me on that wheel:

Intimidation: *Making her afraid by using looks, actions, and gestures. Smashing things. Destroying her property. Abusing pets. Displaying weapons.*

Emotional Abuse: *Putting her down. Making her feel bad about*

123

herself. Calling her names. Making her think she's crazy. Playing mind games. Humiliating her. Making her feel guilty.

Isolation: *Controlling what she does, who she sees, who she talks to, what she reads, and where she goes. Limiting her outside involvement. Using jealousy to justify actions.*

Minimizing Denying and Blaming: *Making light of the abuse and not taking her concerns about it seriously. Saying he abuse didn't happen. Shifting responsibility for abusive behavior. Saying she caused it.*

Economic Abuse: *Preventing her from getting or keeping a job. Making her ask for money. Giving her an allowance. Taking her money. Not letting he know about or have access to family income.*

Male Privilege: *Treating her like a servant: making all the big decisions. Acting like the "Master of the Castle." Being the one to define the roles of a man and a woman.*

Using Children: *Making her feel guilty about the children. Using the children to relay messages. Using visitation to harass her. Threatening to take the children away.*

Coercion and Threats: *Making and/or carrying out threats to do something to her. Threatening to leave her, commit suicide, or report her to welfare. Making her drop charges.* ***Making do illegal things.***

I could clearly see how he manifested every word on the Abuse Wheel. It was almost like watching a movie with an unforeseen hook that gets revealed at the end. I got goose bumps, and a shiver went through my entire body as, for the first time, I fully understood the man I was married to. It was an eye-opener for sure and I wondered how many other women had somehow gotten in similar relationships.

The prosecutors also verified that I would start working for Eric soon since they would ask for restitution, and I had to have employment.

I got to court, flanked by my sister and Stephanie, in good spirits. I had at least twenty handwritten letters from friends and acquaintances who had taken the time out of their day to write good things about my character and the person they knew me to be. I was deeply touched by how they wrote, among other things, what a good mother and person I was.

I soon stood before the judge, and the prosecuting attorney made his recommendations. I was shocked at what was agreed upon but thanked God because things could have gone much worse. In the end, the judge gave me ten years of probation – along with random drug and alcohol tests and a restitution payment of one point four million dollars ($1.4 Million.) I had no idea how I would pay it all, but I had my freedom, which was most important.

I was ordered to register for probation immediately afterward, and my sister and Stephanie told me they would accompany me. I filled out the application, and we waited for my name to be called. Once they called me, I did the fingerprints and DNA test and set up a monthly payment.

I then did an alcohol and drug assessment test through Collin County, and they asked me a series of questions, mostly about drugs and alcohol. The man who conducted them asked me, "So you're charged with money laundering? Did you work for the mob or something?"

I thought working for the mob would have been easier to deal with than Chad. "No, I worked for my husband's construction company, and he got involved with the wrong lenders. It's a long story."

I also had to meet with a lovely lady via Zoom regarding a risk assessment evaluation. She asked me to tell her the number of times I'd been in trouble with the law.

"Never," I answered.

She rolled her eyes and then looked right at me through the screen. "Ma'am, this call is being recorded. If you're lying and we find out, you'll have to do all this again, so tell me the truth."

"I have never been in trouble with the law of any kind." I meet a lot of people on probation, and if you're telling the truth, I'll tell you I'm impressed that a woman of your age was charged with something and has such a squeaky-clean record."

So, my probation is for ten years. I'm at the lowest risk of their repeat offender spectrum, so I do a Zoom once every three months. I'm also at the lowest risk of doing drugs or alcohol, so I only get tested once a year in a bathroom with a female police officer. My restitution is for one point four million dollars.

At times, I wanted to complain to God about how unfair it all was because I never knowingly broke any laws or did anything illegal. But instead of complaining, I would remember all the people who testified against Chad and how badly the prosecutors spoke about both of us; all I could do was be grateful for being able to continue mothering my boys. God continued to be faithful.

CHAPTER TWENTY-FOUR
NEW NORMAL

He got transferred to a prison in Huntsville, where you need permission from the owners of the phones you want to call. The boys talked and concluded that they wouldn't give him access to them. They were hurting for their father, for sure, but they were also angry as they realized the amount of lies he had told them.

I told them it was their decision, and as one of them put it, "Ya, we're over it." I didn't reply. All I knew was if one of my sons said they were over me, I'd be forever devastated. I wondered how Chad felt and realized that already, in his mind, he was most likely blaming me for turning his sons against him. I didn't dwell on the thought; I was over it.

Chad's mother used her status as Power of Attorney for her disgraced son and went to war with me during the divorce. They would not agree on anything. Chad was still trying to call the shots. They wouldn't let me find a buyer for the house and wouldn't sign anything we put in front of him. It got so bad that we had to have an unplanned court date. Chad and his mother stalled on every-thing for so long that when I saw my attorney, I didn't recognize her.

I had hired her in March, and here it was, January – 9 months later – and she looked completely different.

We went to the family courtroom, and I half expected Chad to be there. When he wasn't, I assumed the jail wouldn't pay for a convicted felon to get shackled and transported to a divorce hearing. I was, however, surprised that Chad's mother wasn't there, as his POA. I looked at my lawyer, puzzled, but just then, the judge came in, and we stood at attention. Chad's attorney began by shocking me. "I want to make it clear to the court, Mrs. Carter, and her representation that I will no longer represent Mr. Carter. It's a mutual decision…"

He didn't say why, but I figured it was because of his unreasonable demands and because Chad most likely told his lawyer that he could do his job better than him. I had seen and heard Chad say that to people many times, and I'm sure being in jail for a short time didn't change his demeanor.

My attorney told the judge we were tired of Chad's outrageous demands. They always wanted much more than what was reasonable or rational. I still had to support his two teenage boys, but they didn't seem to care. Whatever the reasons, they were enough for Chad's divorce attorney to stop working for him.

My attorney had to resort to sending paperwork directly to Chad in jail, yet to no avail. He would never reply. We found ourselves in court once again. My attorney told the judge how Chad wasn't responsive and how he had to be the one to find the buyer. He chose a friend of his who was an investor, so he sold the house for much less than what it was worth, depriving me and his kid of large sums of money we could have used and actually needed. He illegally got his truck back, as well as the guns and other items.

The judge asked me how I felt. "I'm over it, your honor. I just want to divorce this man so my boys and I could get on with our lives."

At the end of the day, Chad never signed the divorce papers. I had to pay my attorney to present the case to the judge to sign off on it without his signature. The divorce finally became finalized in June of 2023. It cost me thirty-five thousand dollars ($35,000), which we definitely could have used. My kids were happy for me, for us. Once they saw and heard testimonies of Chad's victims and realized how easily and often he lied to them, they were happy for me to move on.

As for Chad, after his divorce attorney fired him, he hired an appellate lawyer. He still felt he could convince people of his innocence.

As of this writing, Chad has not sent them a letter in a year and a half. I can't fathom being a parent and not continue to try to reach out to their kids. If the roles were reversed, I'd send letters, at least weekly, till the day I died, even if they never replied.

Around the time we sold the house, I took Cole to a Jiu-Jitsu tournament in Waco, Texas. Cole loved to compete, and he participated in all local tournaments. We always had such an amazing time while traveling to each tournament, listening to music, and catching up on life. Those days will always be cherished.

As he was starting to do often, Cole had placed, and we were waiting near the podium for his name to be called. I had seen a guy staring at me, or I thought I did, but I wasn't sure. He looked familiar but I couldn't place where I knew him from or if I knew him. While Cole was accepting his award, the man approached me.

"Excuse me, Mrs. Carter. I just have to tell you that I'm so sorry for what happened to you. I believed you were innocent all along, but the court instructed us that if we let you go, we'd most likely let Chad go, and everyone on the jury did not want to let that man loose to steal from more good people."

I realized this was the jury member with the kind eyes during our trial. I could tell by his face during the trial that he felt terrible for me, and I was right.

"I got outvoted and was very upset. But when I found out you only got probation, I cried like a baby—happy tears, of course."

What were the odds that a jury member would compete in the

129

same Jiu-Jitsu tournament as my son in Waco, Texas on the same day and time? I knew it was no coincidence. God knew I needed to hear those words. I hugged the man and thanked him for telling me what he told me. Then, Cole met him, and we got to meet his wife and children.

It was all so very random but all so very needed. His words impacted me profoundly and brought with them a lot of much-needed inner healing. Once again, God knew what I needed and delivered.

A SPECIAL NOTE FROM THE HEART

Thank you for taking the time to read my story. I must say, from the bottom of my heart, I did not write this book to disparage or put down my ex-husband. Like many other people, he started out with great intentions – loving me and wanting the best for us – but, like many people, he lost his way. I have forgiven him and hope and pray that he finds peace.

Having said that, I want to reiterate my story as a warning to those women who are in relationships with narcissists and to those who aren't in a relationship yet so they can detect the warning signals and never get into that type of relationship.

Beware of **how** people love you. If they **love you too much**, it may be just that – too much! It's not healthy for someone to love you so much that they don't want anyone looking at you, talking to you, or sitting next to you. It's not healthy if someone loves you so much that they want to protect you – when in reality, they are isolating you. It's not healthy when someone loves you so much that they know what's better for you than you.

Sadly, most murders of women were done by men that loved them or used to love them.

Your life is just that – your life. God gave it to you for a special purpose. I assure you that if you find out what that purpose is and commit to making it come true, you'll live a happy, wonderful life.

You are more than your relationship.
You are more than a mother.
You are more than a sister.
You are more than a friend.

You are a wonderful, powerful, and unique human being.

Sincerely,

Shelley Noel

ABOUT THE AUTHOR

Shelley Noel Tollison was born to James Tollison and Debbie Rush on June 22, 1972 in Garland, Texas. James and Debbie were married, but James was never a constant fixture in her life. Their mother, along with the help of her parents, Lena Jo Rush and James Houston Rush, raised her and her older sister Heather Tollison.

Due to her husband's illegal activities, Shelley was charged with Money Laundering and nearly lost her freedom. However, God showed up when all seemed lost.

Today, her desire is to educate women to detect the red flags in narcissistic men before they commit to a long-term relationship that they will not be able to get out of easily. The only easy way for her to get out of her marriage was for God to intervene. He did just that when the state of Texas sentenced him to 45 years in prison and to pay restitution of over $29 million.

 "No matter how bad of a situation you find yourself in, trust in God. Never lose hope that there will be a light at the end of the tunnel."

— SHELLEY NOEL

When she is not speaking to women or working, she enjoys running, walking her dogs, doing yoga, reading, attending concerts, listening to faith-based and motivational podcasts, going to church, and being the best mother she can be to her two sons.

To contact Shelley to speak to your group:
Email: Shelley@shelleynoel.com

 facebook.com/61554101354016
 instagram.com/b_comfa_nt_kning

ACKNOWLEDGEMENTS

First, I would like to thank my sister, Heather: Even though you are only 14 months older than me, you have always been my protector. You are the true version of unconditional love. You put your family over yourself without any hesitation. Thank you for always being there for me, even when I fall. Most importantly, thanks for all the love and support you've given freely my entire life. Love you sis.

My first-born son, Cooper: You have always been a strong, kind, caring and courageous son since you were born. It has been a privilege to call you my son. I am so proud of the man you have become. You have held your head high and surpassed the odds of adversity. I know you will find your path in life. Keep dreaming big! Love you always!

My second born son, Cole: You have always been an adventurous, joyful, competitive, polite and fun-loving son. We had some amazing times together throughout your BJJ competitions. You have found your niche. I know you will excel in whatever you do in life. You do not lose! Follow your dreams! Love you to the moon and back!

My brother-in-law, Anas: You have taken care of my sister since the day you met her. You are an excellent example of what a husband and father should exemplify. You have been so gracious to my boys and me. Thank you for being a big part of my support system.

Ziad, Heidi and Lena: You three are the epitome of selfless kids. You have treated the boys and me like royalty. I am forever grateful for your kindness and unconditional love. I am so blessed to see where life takes you guys in your journey. Love you guys!

My Mom (Debbie): I sure wish you could be here to see the boys and me today. There isn't a day that goes by that I don't think about you. Miss you and love you!

My Grandparents (Mama Jo & Dada): Thank you for helping raise my sister and me. The family gatherings on Sundays will always hold a special place in my heart; watching the Cowboy games and having dinner together. We had a special bond that could never be broken. Miss both of you!

Richard: We have known each other since middle school and when we met back up a couple of years ago it was like no time had passed. You have been my lover, confidant, supporter, caregiver, and best friend for two years now. Thank you for being by my side on some of my darkest days. I'll love you always!

Stephanie F: We met when we were 14 years old in high school. Your friendship means the world to me. Thank you for always being a faithful friend. Anytime I need someone to pray for me or speak positive words into my life, you're my first call. Love you like a sister.

Stacie: Since I first met you in art class in middle school. Your friendship has never wavered. You are the kind of friend that will always be by my side in the good and bad times. I cherish you and I am proud to call you my lifelong friend!

Kathy: You are one of my closest lifelong friends. We were both pregnant at the same time and shared a connection that can't be replaced or broken. Thank you for always being in my corner during the ups and downs of life. Love you friend.

Ashley: You are such a sweet soul who treated my boys and me like family. Thank you for assisting me for 10 years in some of the most difficult times in our lives. I am so proud of the woman, mom, wife, and friend you have always been and will be in the years to come.

Eli: You are an amazing ghostwriter. Thank you for guiding me through the process of writing a book and publishing it. I am forever thankful that God put you in my life when I needed someone to help me tell my story.

Tara M: You are my newest friend in my inner circle but it feels like we have been friends for a lifetime. Thank you for being someone I can confide in and trust to give me the truth even if it isn't what I want to hear. You have been one of my biggest supporters. I am forever grateful for our friendship. I am proud of the person who you have become over the last several years.